U.S. AIR POWER

AUTHOR:
BILL YENNE

PHOTOGRAPHER:
GEORGE HALL

Publications
International, Ltd.

CONTENTS

WINGS 4

FIGHTERS 8
F-4 PHANTOM II 12
F-5 TIGER II 24
F-14 TOMCAT 32
F-15 EAGLE 54
F-16 FIGHTING FALCON 72
F/A-18 HORNET 94

ATTACK PLANES 116
A-4 SKYHAWK 120
A-6 INTRUDER 130
AV-8B HARRIER II 146
A-7 CORSAIR II 158
A-10 THUNDERBOLT II 166

BOMBERS 176
B-52 STRATOFORTRESS 180
F-111/FB-111 AARDVARK 188
B-1 198
P-3 ORION 208
B-2 "STEALTH" 218

**RECONNAISSANCE AND
ELECTRONIC WARFARE AIRCRAFT** 220
U-2/TR-1 SERIES 224

SR-71 BLACKBIRD 228
E-2 HAWKEYE 236
E-3 SENTRY 240
EF-111 RAVEN 244

TRANSPORTS 246
C-130 HERCULES 250
C-141 STARLIFTER 258
C-5 GALAXY 262

AERIAL TANKERS 268
KC-135 STRATOTANKER 272
KC-10 EXTENDER 280

**UTILITY AND TRANSPORT
HELICOPTERS** 282
UH-1 HUEY (IROQUOIS) 286
HH-3 JOLLY GREEN GIANT/CH-53
SEA STALLION 288
CH-47 CHINOOK 294
H-60 BLACK HAWK/NIGHT HAWK/
SEAHAWK 296

ATTACK HELICOPTERS 300
AH-1 HUEYCOBRA/SUPERCOBRA 304
OH-6 CAYUSE/DEFENDER 310
AH-64 APACHE 314

Louis Weber, C.E.O.
Publications International, Ltd.
7373 North Cicero Avenue
Lincolnwood, Illinois 60646

Permission is never granted for commercial purposes.
Printed and bound in Yugoslavia.

h g f e d c b a

Library of Congress Card Number: 88-63611

*Front cover photos
(clockwise from left):*
F/18 Blue Angels, 5-15 Eagle, B-2 Stealth,
(UPI/BETTMANN NEWSPHOTOS),
AH-1 Cobra, F-15 pilot.

Back cover photos: (top)
F-4 Phantom, *(bottom)* F-16.

ISBN 0-88176-531-7

Preceding page: RF-4C
Phantom. *Left:* A-7 Corsair II
(top), A6-E Intruder *(center),*
F/A-18 Hornet *(bottom).*
Below: F-16 trainer.

WINGS

The all-weather A-6 Intruder.

FIGHTERS

**Three Naval Reserve
F/A-18 Hornets.**

The crew of an F-4 slides its
bird into position beneath
a tanker for refueling.

Right: Maintenance of an Air
Guard RF-4 at Birmingham,
Louisiana.

The Marines enjoyed a long, successful relationship with the Phantom, but the big bird is being phased out of the Corps except for RF-4B variants and in the Reserves.

Marine Corps reservists out of NAS Dallas fire up their aged Phantom at Kaneohe, Hawaii.

Plane captain readies a Marine F-4 for a predawn Red Flag hop at Nellis AFB, Nevada.

F-5
TIGER II

The Northrop F-5 series was never intended to serve with American forces. The F-5s that now do serve with the U.S. Navy and Air Force pretend that they are the enemy.

The original idea behind the F-5 back in the late 1950s was to develop the cheapest possible supersonic fighter—a jet fighter that the U.S. government could buy at low cost and transfer to allied nations under the Military Assistance Program (MAP). Today, however, the F-5 also serves with the Navy's and Air Force's "aggressor" squadrons.

Northrop's Model N-156 was selected for the MAP contract and given the nickname "Freedom Fighter." Northrop based the N-156 on their T-38 supersonic trainer program, and the two aircraft are, therefore, strikingly similar in appearance. The first N-156 prototype was ready in 1957, but intragovernmental disagreement over the parameters of the program kept the Freedom Fighter, officially designated F-5, out of production for four years.

By September 1964, a number of F-5s were at Williams AFB, Arizona, where pilots from many nations were anxious to make them their own. Iran and South Korea were first, followed by the Philippines and Taiwan. The Freedom Fighter's baptism of fire came in 1965; American pilots took them into combat in Vietnam prior to turning them over to the South Vietnamese Air Force. Pakistan and Libya received F-5s under the MAP, as did such NATO countries as Norway, the Netherlands, Greece, and Turkey. In terms of cost, the Freedom Fighter concept was a success, because the F-5 sold for less than one-third the price of the contemporary F-4 Phantom II. Neutral Switzerland bought the F-5, making it the only jet fighter that country ever purchased from the United States. Switzerland was among just a handful of nations to actually buy the F-5. North of the border, Canadair obtained a license to build them under the CF-5 designation for the Canadian Air Force. Canadair eventually sold some Canadian-built CF-5s to the Netherlands as NF-5s.

The name "Tiger" evolved in the Far East, where F-5s were known as "Skoshi Tiger," or "Little Tiger," because of their size and tenacity. In fact, Skoshi Tiger had been the code name for the deployment of F-5s to Vietnam. The name Tiger became an official appellation of the airplane itself only after the F-5E (and dual-control F-5F), introduced in 1973, was called "Tiger II." More than 1,200 F-5As and dual control F-5Bs were built, and more than 1,400 F-5E and F-5F Tiger IIs were built through 1987.

In 1980, Northrop began developing an even more advanced F-5, which had increased weapons capability, all new avionics, and the most advanced radar system in the world. Although similar to the Tiger II (except for a redesigned nose and tailplane), the new aircraft was vastly more capable. Originally designated F-5G, the new plane—already named Tigershark—proved to be so much of an advancement over the Tiger II that it was redesignated F-20. The Tigershark has the fastest scramble time (from the moment the alarm sounds to "gear in the wells") in the world.

The Tigershark's story is one of the most unusual in aviation history. Northrop spent $1.2 billion developing what was one of the most advanced aircraft in the world, then built three examples, logged 1,534 demonstration flights all over the world between 1982 and 1986, but failed to sell a single airplane to anybody, anywhere!

With such a low-cost, high-performance fighter, Northrop should have had customers banging their door down to buy them. But this never happened. Many of the old F-5 customers showed interest, but not one crossed the line. The U.S. Air Force even strongly considered the F-20 for its new lightweight air defense fighter. In November 1986, when the Air Force chose the F-16 over the F-20, the handwriting was on the wall, and Northrop decided to cut its losses and mothball the whole program.

The Air Force has always been a rather poor customer for F-5s in general. They bought a majority of the original F-5s, but mostly for export. There were no operational F-5 units in the Air Force until 1975 when that service found itself with over one hundred F-5s that couldn't be delivered to the South Vietnamese Air Force because South Vietnam had ceased to exist.

It was at about this same time that both the Navy and the Air Force came up with the idea of *dissimilar* air-to-air combat training. Most fighter pilots had engaged in mock aerial combat with *familiar* aircraft, usually with aircraft like those that the pilots themselves were flying.

(continued on p. 27)

***Right:* The Northrop F-5E Tiger is a small, simple fighter designed and built for the world export market.**

A captive Sidewinder missile gives the pilot all the realistic firing cues, including the distinctive growl that signals a good "lock." But it's not a real missile, lacking a warhead and a rocket motor.

A Naval Reserve Tomcat of the VF-302 "Stallions" fires an AIM-7 Sparrow radar-guided missile in a rare live-fire exercise.

Left: Tomcats assigned to Miramar's VF-111 "Sundowners." *Above, top:* Tomcat crews sit through exhaustive briefs and debriefs that typically last far longer than the dogfights themselves. *Above, bottom:* A Naval Reserve Tomcat takes on a load of activè Sparrow and Sidewinder air-to-air missiles for a live-fire exercise over the Pacific Missile Test Range off San Diego.

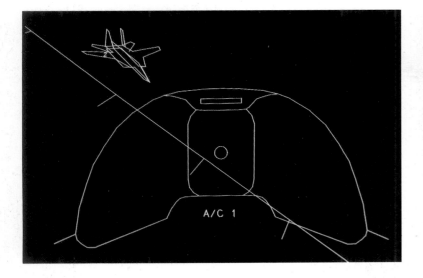

Above, top: Pilot's-eye view of a dogfight artificially recreated by the computerized ACMI (Air Combat Maneuvering Instrumentation) system. The system records an entire aerial engagement for later debriefing. *Above, bottom:* Actual pilot's view from Tomcat front seat. *Right:* The Pacific coast slides beneath a tight formation of Tomcats.

The two-crew Tomcat is a huge fighter by any measure, probably the world's largest single-role fighter aircraft.

Maximum takeoff weight of an F-14 approaches 30 tons.

F-15 EAGLE

The McDonnell Douglas F-15 Eagle is the best air-superiority fighter in the world. Some people may take exception to that notion, but certainly none of them could have been anywhere near Lebanon's Bekaa valley in June 1982, when Israeli F-15s, while fighting the Syrian Air Force, tackled the best Soviet-built fighters and smoked 80 of them for the loss of nary an F-15.

Nowhere is the inherent prowess of the Eagle better known than among the pilots who fly them, which is why "Eagle drivers" are frequently known as "ego drivers."

The F-15 is to the U.S. Air Force what the F-14 is to the U.S. Navy: the leading edge of fighter technology as defined by the mission requirements of that particular service. The F-15 flies from a multitude of places, but its drivers must always be ready to fly from unfamiliar fields. U.S. Air Force F-15s are based within striking distance of potential world conflict. They are stationed in Germany and Iceland as an integral part of the American commitment to NATO, and in Okinawa, where they serve to provide air defense coverage to South Korea and Japan. In Alaska they fly for the U.S. Air Force's Alaskan Air Command (AAC), whose motto, "Top Cover for America," literally describes the F-15's role on the Arctic frontier.

The 5,000-mile arc defined by the AAC motto is no idle venue when Soviet bomber bases are just 30 minutes flying time from the 49th state. During 1987 and the first part of 1988, for example, the Soviet Air Force was running nuclear-strike training missions against Alaska at the rate of more than one per week, compared with less than once a month in the years before Mikhail Gorbachev took over as premier. These forays become cat-and-mouse exercises in which AAC Eagles must intercept the Soviet Tu-95 Bear bombers before they reach U.S. territory. If the F-15s don't succeed in waggling their wings in front of the nose of the big silver Bears over international waters, the Russians will probably turn back anyway, but they'll turn back knowing they weren't *forced* back. Such is day-to-day life on the front lines of the Cold War.

The missions flown by AAC Eagle drivers are exactly what the Air Force had in mind when it gave the McDonnell component of McDonnell Douglas the green light to develop a follow-up to the F-4 Phantom. The idea was to take everything that had been learned in air-to-air combat in Vietnam, add the best that modern, emerging electronics technology had to offer, and build the best possible fighter to fulfill the Air Force mission. The first of the Eagles flew in July 1972, and the first F-15As entered squadron service four years later. The F-15C followed in 1979. By the early 1980s, Eagles had already begun to replace the F-4s as the Air Force's first-line fighters. In the meantime, export deals were struck in which Eagles would be exported to Israel, Japan, and Saudi Arabia.

Unlike the F-4, McDonnell designed the F-15 as a one-person plane, with the role of the backseater performed by a high-speed computer that simply wasn't available 20 or 30 years ago. Two-seat combat-capable F-15B and F-15D trainers do exist but, for the most part, the Eagle drivers ride alone.

The Eagle's armament includes the 20-millimeter cannon that was unfortunately omitted on the early F-4s, as well as the AIM-7 Sparrow and AIM-9 Sidewinder air-to-air missiles (which are common to the F-4). The more sophisticated AIM-120 AMRAAM is also included. In 1984, two squadrons of F-15s were experimentally equipped with the ALMV/ASAT, a two-stage missile that could be fired into space to destroy satellites. After a successful test in 1985, Congress banned further testing or deployment of the system.

In 1987, the Air Force began taking deliveries of the F-15E, a long-range, two-seat fighter-bomber based on the F-15D. The speed and maneuverability of the Eagle had made it the ideal airframe to adapt as the 21st century replacement for the aging F-111 fighter-bomber fleet. While the onrush of aviation technology will probably see the F-15C replaced as the Air Force's top air-superiority fighter by the turn of the century, the F-15E will probably be trucking bombs for another quarter century.

McDONNELL DOUGLAS F-15C EAGLE

Wingspan:	42 ft. 9¾ in.
Length:	63 ft. 9 in.
Height:	18 ft. 5½ in.
Engines:	two Pratt & Whitney F100-PW-100 turbofans
Engine thrust (lbs.):	23,830
Maximum T-O weight (lbs.):	68,000
Operating altitude (ft.):	60,000
Top speed (mph):	Mach 2.5 +
Maximum range (miles):	3,570

Right: **An Eagle over the New Orleans Superdome.**

Left: The tremendous energy of an F-15 permits vertical acceleration when fuel and weapons loads are not too great. *Above:* The Eagle, like the Tomcat, is very large for a fighter but is only a one-seater. *Right:* The photographer catches a self-portrait in rear seat of an F-15B.

Left: The F-15 Eagle has the wing technology and power to turn and fight with much smaller adversaries. *Above, top and bottom:* Bitburg Eagles are frequently loaded with a maximum complement of four medium-range Sparrow missiles and four smaller heat-seeking Sidewinders.

A two-seat F-15B in a mock dogfight over the Gulf of Mexico.

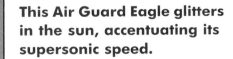

This Air Guard Eagle glitters in the sun, accentuating its supersonic speed.

Eagles of the Louisiana Air National Guard against a setting sun south of New Orleans.

Fully loaded Eagles out of Bitburg, Germany, patrol the East-West border. Each carries a maximum air-combat load of four Sparrow radar-guided missiles and four heat-seeking Sidewinders for the close-in fight.

Above: F-15s share an assembly line with F/A-18 Hornets and AV-8B Harriers at the huge McDonnell-Douglas plant in St. Louis. *Right:* A Louisiana Guard Eagle carrying a towable target dart for live-firing practice with the 20-millimeter cannon carried in each jet. The target is towed a mile behind the plane and contains a microphone that records near misses of bullets for later tally.

An F-15 Eagle silhouetted against a Florida evening sky.

Brightly painted F-16s announce the arrival of the *Thunderbirds*.

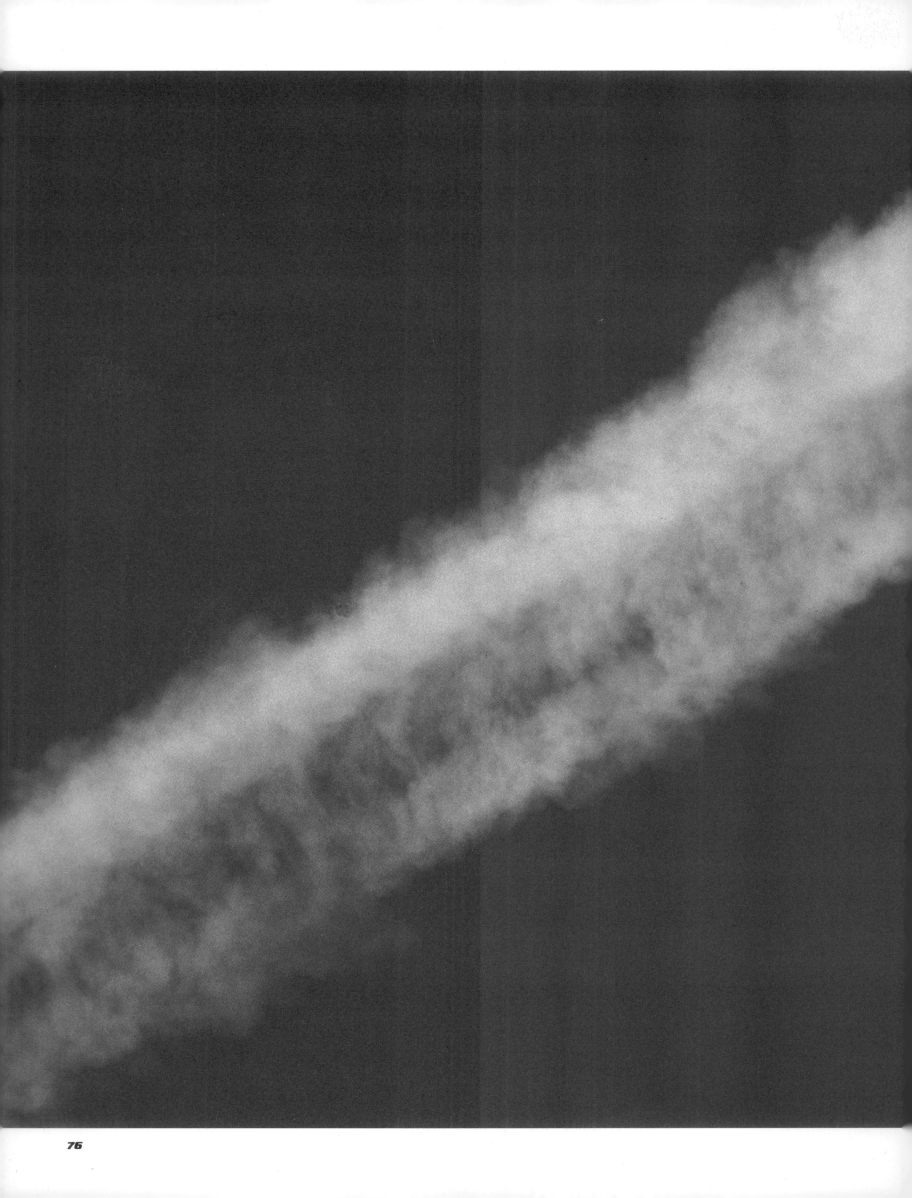

Left: The Air Force *Thunderbirds* perform with impeccable precision, requiring much practice and highly skilled pilots. *Above:* The *Thunderbirds* are based at Nellis AFB, Nevada.

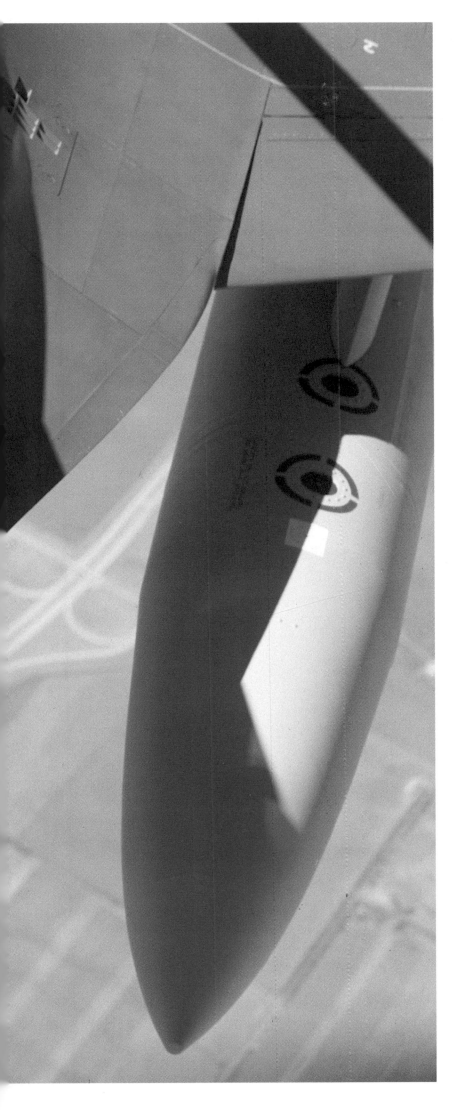

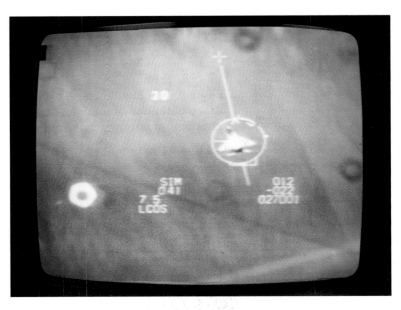

Left: **A Falcon driver is photographed from a tanker while gassing up.** *Above, top:* **The F-16 pilot's left hand controls engine throttle and various radar and weapons switches, of which there are more than one per finger.** *Above, bottom:* **Most teen fighters carry videotape setups to record details of the entire hop for later debriefing. Here a Falcon tracks and fires at a hapless Eagle.**

A Falcon out of Hahn Air
Base, Germany, practices
low-level flying.

Left: An Air Force Reserve Falcon driver mounts up for an evening hop at Hill AFB, Utah. *Above:* The good-looking F-16 is about as small as a modern full-capability fighter-bomber can be.

The F-16 is a jack-of-all-trades: interceptor, attacker, or part of the *Thunderbirds*.

Two F-16s from the 419th TAC Fighter Group, Air Force Reserve, at day's end over western Utah.

A brand-new F-16, en route from the factory to Germany, slides away from a tanker after the first of six refuelings during the trans-ocean ride.

A Falcon awaits its pilot for a night hop. The little fighter normally carries two Sidewinder missiles on wingtips for aerial combat.

F/A-18
HORNET

It was actually born as the Northrop YF-17, and to-day it may be called F-18 *or* A-18, depending on who's flying it. The Hornet is to the U.S. Navy and Marine Corps what the F-16 is to the Air Force: a small, relatively low-cost, single-engine jet that can perform a variety of jobs from fighter to fighter-bomber. The biggest difference is that the F/A-18 is a two-engine aircraft, which is now required by the Navy for its carrier aircraft because of the safety factor on long-distance missions over the world's vast, empty oceans. If you lose one engine, you still have one more.

The F/A-18 is a direct derivative of the YF-17 that Northrop developed to compete for the Air Force contract that was ultimately won in 1974 by the F-16. When the YF-17 lost, McDonnell Douglas acquired the blueprints, brought Northrop in as a major subcontractor, and undertook a major redesign. This proposal was in turn bought by the Navy to satisfy its dual requirements for a carrier-based attack plane and a new fighter for the Marine Corps. The former was designated as A-18 and the latter as F-18, but they were the same plane.

The new F/A-18 was first flown in November 1978, and made its first flights from a carrier 11 months later on the USS *America.* Australia and Canada also selected the Hornet for many of the same reasons that the U.S. Navy bought it. Cost and versatility were factors, as was the fact of its having two engines. Australia, like the U.S. Navy, has a lot of ocean to patrol, and Canada has a vast, harsh, sparsely populated land mass to patrol. Another factor in Canada's choice of the Hornet (which they have designated CF-18) over the F-16 was that Canada—like the U.S. Navy—uses the "hose & drogue" method of aerial refueling, rather than the "flying boom" method used by the U.S. Air Force. Since the Hornet was already designed with this in mind, the CF-18s didn't have to be retrofitted with a different type of refueling equipment.

The armament of the Hornet is as diverse as that of the Falcon. It carries the 20-millimeter cannon, which is mounted on the top center of the nose rather than at the side of the fuselage like those of the F-14, F-15, and F-16. In fighter configuration, the Hornet, like the Falcon, carries AIM-9 Sidewinder air-to-air missiles on wingtip racks, while a variety of other equipment, such as the AIM-7 Sparrow, can be carried underwing. For attack/fighter-bomber missions, the F/A-18 Hornet's armor-er selects from conventional or nuclear bombs, and AGM-88 HARM antiradar missiles or AGM-65 Maverick air-to-ground missiles.

For its naval attack mission, the Hornet can also carry the AGM-109 Harpoon sea-skimming, antiship missile, which is the U.S. Navy equivalent of the French-built Exocet that caused so much trouble for the British Navy in the Falklands and the U.S. Navy in the Persian Gulf.

When projecting the future role of the Hornet, the Marine Corps motto "First to Fight" comes to mind. The present, highly fluid nature of geopolitical troubles has placed the Navy and the Marine Corps on the leading edge of American projection of its military power world-wide. If push comes to shove and the United States must "send in the Marines," the F/A-18 will be among the choices for a first echelon of air support for them.

McDONNELL DOUGLAS F/A-18

Wingspan:	37 ft. 6 in.
Length:	56 ft.
Height:	15 ft. 3½ in.
Engines:	two General Electric F404-GE-400 turbofans
Engine thrust (lbs.):	16,000
Maximum T-O weight (lbs.):	36,710
Operating altitude (ft.):	50,000
Top speed (mph):	Mach 1.8+
Maximum range (miles):	2,303

Right: **The dual-role F/A-18 typically carries bombs for ground-attack missions and wingtip Sidewinder missiles for air-to-air dogfights.**

The front view of a Hornet shows unique canted twin vertical stabilizers.

A dogfighting Hornet over the Great Salt Lake.

Left: An F-18 loaded with 500-pound bombs rolls in on its unlucky target.

Above: Carrier-deck ordnancemen upload Sidewinders onto the wing pylon of a Hornet.

Left: Plane captain helps the pilot strap into his F-18. **Above, top:** The digital electronic panel of the F-18, with radar screen at right and terrain map screen at bottom center. **Above, center:** The F-18 pilot's view of his wingmen through the windscreen Head-Up Display (HUD). **Above, bottom:** The Marine F-18 slings Sidewinders on wingtip and underwing stations.

A Navy Hornet ripple-fires 5-inch ZUNI rockets over the Fallon, Nevada, bombing range.

Left: Impeccably positioned F/A-18s of the *Blue Angels* flight demonstration team await their pilots. *Above:* The *Blue Angels* insignia appears on each jet.

Tight *Blue Angels* four-ship, with only three feet of separation between wingtips.

Above: Blue Angels plane captain salutes his pilot during ceremonial "walk-down." *Right:* Lead and slot aircraft are inverted in this crowd-pleasing pass.

A Navy Hornet is propelled off the carrier deck by a steam-powered catapult. The jet accelerates from 0-150 mph in two seconds!

A quartet of Hornets sucks
it in tight over the Gulf
of Mexico.

Marine Hornet driver Capt. Tim "Tiny" Timm (tiny at 6'4") poses with his Hornet.

Three wingmen in tight formation pursue a Hornet that has a rear-looking remote pod camera mounted on its underwing weapons station.

A Navy A-7 Corsair lights off a 5-inch ZUNI rocket.

Despite its ugliness and shape (it almost looks as if it is flying backward), the A-6 is a strong and capable attack/bomber.

Attack planes have been the answer to many a prayer murmured nervously by a Marine or GI stuck in an artillery-pounded foxhole.

Attack planes don't have the speed and dash of fighters nor the huge weapons capacity of bombers. Attack planes function at the behest of ground forces. Such missions are flown by fighter-bombers as well as attack planes, but the latter are designed specifically for supporting surface forces. (The term "surface" is used because attack aircraft operate against land and sea targets.) The Navy's carrier-based attackers are responsible for bombing land targets for Marine Corps operations ashore and for attacking enemy ships or submarines in support of friendly vessels or on-shore positions.

Against ground targets, the attack role may take three forms. The first is *close air support,* where the aircraft is within a one-mile radius (or less) of the troops it's supporting. The second is *battlefield interdiction,* where the aircraft is attacking targets, such as tanks, that are in the general area but not yet engaged with friendly forces. The third is *deep interdiction,* where an attack bomber flies up to 500 miles into enemy territory to attack targets, such as bridges, airfields, and choke-points, which may not have an immediate relation to the current battle, but whose destruction can prevent reinforcements from reaching the battlefield. Although deep interdiction is a role that attack planes share with fighter-bombers, very deep interdiction, 1,500 miles or more, falls to aircraft that have the electronic countermeasure capability to defend against layers of radar and anti-aircraft weapons.

Generally, attack planes are the slowest of combat aircraft, although there are exceptions. Pound for pound, though, attack planes generally carry the greatest relative weapons load. This load can include a variety of air-to-ground ordnance, ranging from simple high-explosive bombs to complex radar-guided "smart" bombs or special delayed-action munitions specifically designed to destroy thick concrete bunkers or put deep craters into runways. Air-to-ground missiles (AGM) are also part of the arsenal, and each is tailored for a particular task.

Attack squadrons are organized in a way that generally parallels that of fighter squadrons. Aboard each of the Navy's 14 carriers is a carrier air wing (CVW) with two fighter squadrons (VF) and an assortment of about three attack squadrons (VA) that fly A-6s and A-7s. Some of these are being transformed into strike-fighter squadrons (VFA), organized around the F/A-18.

The Air Force has designated its attack squadrons as fighter squadrons and has distributed them throughout the world as part of the four tactical combat commands: the Tactical Air Command (TAC), the Alaskan Air Command (AAC), the U.S. Air Forces in Europe (USAFE), and the Pacific Air Forces (PACAF). Of the roughly 500 attack planes in the Air Force, 90 percent are A-10s.

It is axiomatic in modern warfare that air power is a vital component of any winning team. There is no phase of modern warfare where the air power/land power teamwork is more evident or more important than when a ground commander calls upon the air commander to send in the attack planes.

A-4
SKYHAWK

When the Skyhawk first flew, they called it a "hot rod." The Skyhawk was fast and trim—everything an attack plane had never been—and it weighed less, while carrying a greater bomb load, than the "dump truck" attack bombers of the Korean War.

The idea behind the Skyhawk was for maximum punch with minimum weight in a small-size attack bomber for use on the U.S. Navy's carriers. Designed by Douglas Aircraft Company ace designer Ed Heinemann, the "Hot Rod" Skyhawk first flew under the A4D designation in 1954. It weighed four tons empty, but it could *carry* three tons of weapons, including nuclear weapons. In production for an incredible quarter of a century, a total of 2,960 Skyhawks rolled off the Douglas assembly line before production ceased. Its designation was changed from A4D to the multiservice A-4 in 1962.

Two years later, the Skyhawk went to war. In August 1964, when American ships were attacked by North Vietnamese patrol boats, A-4s were among the first American aircraft to participate in the counterstrike. Skyhawks continued to play an important role as part of the U.S. Navy strike force throughout the duration of the war.

A-4s were among the first American warplanes transferred to Israel, and although they didn't arrive in time to be part of the action in the Six-Day War of June 1967, they did take part in the low-level "war of attrition" between Israel and Egypt after 1969 and in the Yom Kippur War of October 1973.

The only American warplane since World War II to serve three different nations in three completely different conflicts, the Skyhawk went to war a third time in 1982. In May of that year, Skyhawks of the Argentine Navy and Air Force were deployed to attack British forces attempting to retake the Falkland Islands, which Argentina had invaded in April. Operating valiantly at the limit of their range, the Argentine A-4s succeeded in sinking two British frigates and a destroyer before the British were able to recapture the islands.

After seeing nearly a decade of combat in Vietnam, the A-4 continued in U.S. Navy service until 1987, during which time Skyhawks were assigned to be used by the Navy's world renowned *Blue Angels* aerobatic team.

Still in service today with U.S. Marine attack squadrons (as well as with Israel and Argentina), the Skyhawk remains a tireless, heavy-hitting war bird. Equipped with a 20-millimeter cannon and AIM-9 Sidewinders for air defense, the A-4 can also carry a variety of air-to-ground munitions as part of its three-ton load. These include "iron" bombs, radar-guided "smart" bombs, the likes of the AGM-62 Walleye television-guided missile and the AGM-65 Maverick, and launchers for unguided 2.75-inch rockets. Israeli Skyhawks can also carry Gabriel 3 anti-ship missiles and Rafael Shafrir air-to-air missiles.

Another system, originally developed by the U.S. Navy but now in use by Israel and the U.S. Marines, is a "buddy" refueling system by which Skyhawks can refuel one another in an emergency.

In almost any other context, it would be hard to imagine an attack plane being part of an aerobatic team like the *Blue Angels.* However, because of the Skyhawk's stunning maneuverability, there is little to wonder about, and it is easy to picture how and why these remarkable little planes have been so effective for so many air services for so many years.

DOUGLAS A-4F SKYHAWK

Wingspan:	27 ft. 6 in.
Length:	41 ft. 4 in.
Height:	15 ft.
Engine:	one Pratt & Whitney J52-P8A turbojet
Engine thrust (lbs.):	9,300
Gross weight (lbs.):	19,356
Operating altitude (ft.):	58,600
Top speed (mph):	646 (loaded)
Maximum range (miles):	2,000

Right: **Four Marine Corps A-4Ms fly behind a refueling tanker over Southern California.**

Top Gun instructors fly souped-up Skyhawks stripped of excess weight and stuffed with big Pratt & Whitney P-8 engines. This Skyhawk variant is nick-named "Mongoose."

Above: Mark 82 500-pound bombs on the wing station of a Marine A-4M. *Right:* The A-4 Skyhawk has been in active service for 30 years; the Marines still operate them as solid light-attack bombers. The hump behind the pilot contains electronic countermeasures equipment.

Left: An elegant delta formation of six *Blue Angels* Skyhawks. *Above:* The Navy's *Blue Angels* flew Skyhawks for a decade before switching to the F/A-18 in 1987.

Left: **Navy and Marine Corps jet pilots still do their advanced flight training in 2-seat TA-4 Skyhawks.**
Right: **Adversary squadron VF-127, based at Fallon, Nevada, flies A-4s painted a variety of camouflage schemes.**

A-6
INTRUDER

There's one in every crowd—and in this case, there's one A-6 squadron on every U.S. Navy carrier. Built by Grumman, the preeminent builder of American carrier-based aircraft for the last half century, the Intruder was first flown in April 1960; new Intruder acquisitions are still part of the Navy's budget.

The Intruder grew out of the Navy's need for an all-weather attack plane with an eight-ton bomb load to support both Navy and Marine Corps operations. The basic version was the A-6A, of which 484 were built. Many of these were, in turn, converted or adapted for roles other than ground attack.

Today, the A-6E is the Navy's standard "medium-attack" aircraft, although with a nine-ton bomb load, *medium* is hardly an adjective that a nest of bad guys taking pot shots at Marines would be likely to use if an Intruder intruded upon them!

The A-6E was born in 1970 as a converted A-6A. This variant evolved into the A-6E/TRAM (Target Recognition and Attack Multisensor) standard by 1980, to which all previous A-6Es were converted and to which all current production types are built. TRAM is really a whole basket of electronics that make the A-6E's job easy and its role more efficient. The "basket" itself is a turret located under the nose that carries both infrared- and laser-targeting sensors and multimode radar. The lasers are used in conjunction with laser-guided weapons. The TRAM system is multifaceted in that if one A-6E spots a target with its laser and can't fire for some reason, a second A-6E can launch its weapons against the target using the first A-6E's laser as a guide. In addition to laser-guided munitions, the A-6E can carry "iron" bombs and AGM-84 Harpoon antiship missiles. The A-6E can pack Sidewinders to defend itself from hostile aircraft.

A second important A-6 variant in service with the U.S. Navy today is the EA-6B. This special electronic-warfare version is called "Prowler" rather than Intruder. The Prowler accompanies an A-6E strike force and uses highly sophisticated electronics to jam enemy radar that may be trying to locate the strike force or guide anti-aircraft missiles against the attacking Intruders.

The Intruder carries its two-person crew in a side-by-side seating arrangement typical of much larger planes. The pilot occupies the left seat, with the weapons system operator/navigator on the right. The Prowler is five feet longer than the Intruder in order to accommodate an additional pair of crew members who operate the electronic-countermeasures hardware.

Any attack mission flown by Intruders against a target protected by radar-directed missiles—especially enemy surface ships—would involve a Prowler riding herd to confuse the enemy and give the A-6Es a chance to slip in and do their work. The Intruder/Prowler team, because they have basically similar airframes, are an ideal combination to have aboard a carrier from the standpoint of maintenance, as well as operations. They are indeed a "deadly duo" that can efficiently confuse radar and eliminate targets in one fast, smooth stroke.

GRUMMAN A-6E INTRUDER

Wingspan:	53 ft.
Length:	54 ft. 9 in.
Height:	16 ft. 2 in.
Engines:	two Pratt & Whitney J52-P-8B turbojets
Engine thrust (lbs.):	9,300
Maximum T-O weight (lbs.):	60,400
Operating altitude (ft.):	42,400
Cruising speed (mph):	474
Top speed (mph):	806
Maximum range (miles):	2,740

Right: **The nonretractable refueling probe of the A-6 curves into the sky in front of the crew. Note its slight cant to the pilot's right.**

The A-6E Intruder is the carrier's heavy bomber, with a bomb load approaching nine tons.

An A-6 unloads 500-pound bombs with retarders over the Fallon, Nevada, range.

An Intruder lets fly with 5-inch ZUNI rockets.

The Intruder is readily identified by its bulbous front end and pointed tail section.

An A-6E, part of a carrier's combat arsenal, tightly secured on deck.

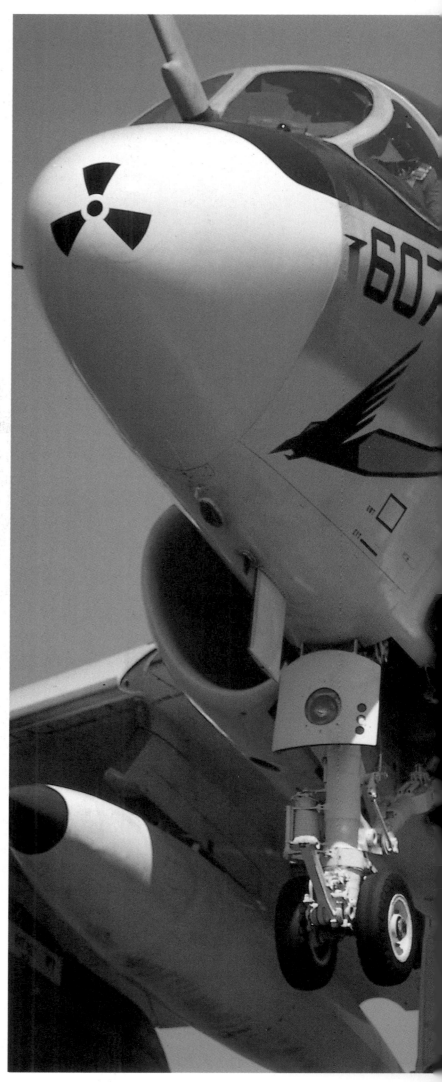

Above, top: The Intruder is crewed by two. *Above, bottom:* Support crew upload electronic-jamming equipment onto an EA-6B Prowler, a variant of the Intruder. *Right:* The Prowler can accomodate two extra crewmembers.

145

AV-8B HARRIER II

Picture an airplane that can take off *straight up* and then hover in midair like a helicopter. Picture an airplane with a turning radius *shorter than itself.* Picture an airplane that, when pursued by another airplane, can *stop in midair,* let the enemy overshoot it, and then accelerate and shoot the enemy down. This is the Harrier.

Beginning immediately after World War II, a number of countries undertook studies to develop a combat aircraft that could take off and land like a helicopter without compromising any airplanelike performance when airborne. Helicopters could take off vertically, but they were slow, delicate, lumbering creatures in the air.

Success was finally achieved in 1960 by Hawker aircraft in England, with the test flight of their P.1127. Put into production under the name Kestrel, these aircraft were not everything that was hoped for, but they were the first operational Vertical Takeoff and Landing (VTOL) aircraft in the world. By 1968, the Kestrel had evolved into the Harrier, which was a much more practical and versatile VTOL bird. The following year, Royal Air Force Harriers took part in the *Daily Mail* London-to-New York race. Although the six-hour time was no speed record, it was presentable, and the Harrier was the only plane in the race to land *in* Manhattan.

These VTOL capabilities very much interested the U.S. Marine Corps, which was keen on the idea of fast attack aircraft that could take off anywhere. By using such an airplane, they could carry their own air power on an assault ship and not have to depend on an aircraft carrier for air support when making an amphibious landing. The Marines ordered 110 Harriers, which went into service in 1971 under the designation AV-8A. In 1975, McDonnell Douglas undertook the task of developing an improved Harrier with a larger wing that could double the range and payload of the AV-8A. This project resulted in the AV-8B prototype, which first flew in 1978. In 1982, a joint manufacturing agreement was entered into, whereby British Aerospace (which had absorbed Hawker) and McDonnell Douglas would produce a VTOL aircraft that would be known as Harrier II.

In 1975, at the same time that the U.S. Marines were looking at the Harrier, the British Royal Navy also decided to buy a variant called Sea Harrier. The Royal Navy wanted to give up on full-size aircraft carriers to save money. The Royal Navy still needed the flexibility that carriers afforded. The Sea Harrier was the ideal solution.

By using them, the Royal Navy could get by with carriers one-fourth the size of a typical U.S. Navy carrier. Sea Harriers could operate in the VTOL mode from any flat surface, but when they used the STOL (Short Takeoff and Landing) mode on a short flight deck, they saved fuel and thus increased their range.

The vindication of the Sea Harrier/small carrier concept came in 1982. In April of that year, Argentina invaded and captured the British-owned Falkland Islands in the South Atlantic. Because there were no airfields nearby that could be used by either fighters or attack planes, the British were faced with the task of retaking the islands without any air power except their Harriers. The Sea Harriers, augmented by RAF Harriers, were the entire air-power element of the British effort to recapture the Falklands. The trusty "jump jets" proved themselves to be more important and more reliable than anyone could have predicted. Indeed, the Harriers were the most important weapons of the short-lived war. Not only did they fly more than 2,000 attack missions but, when pressed into service as fighters, they shot down at least 20 enemy aircraft without one loss in air-to-air combat.

Today's U.S. Marine Corps AV-8B Harrier would fly and fight in much the same way the English jump jets did in the Falklands: in support of a joint Navy/Marines amphibious assault or in the context of Marine operations ashore. While the Royal Navy has but four assault ships that host Harriers, the U.S. Navy has about 60 equivalent ships. Normally, Marine Corps operations from one of these assault carriers involves the use of helicopters, but Harriers routinely are deployed for training exercises aboard many of these ships.

The Marine Corps AV-8B is armed with a 25-millimeter cannon, and the McDonnell Douglas wing of the AV-8B gives it a potential of carrying a four-ton bomb load, compared with 2.5 tons for the AV-8A. In addition to bombs, the AV-8B can be configured to carry a variety of guided air-to-ground munitions and—as the British

(continued on p. 148)

Right: **The only American operators of the British-designed Harrier are the Marines, who use it as a fast-response light attack jet.**

(continued from p. 146)

found so useful in the Falklands—AIM-9 Sidewinder air-to-air missiles.

Despite its demonstrated success and the success of the V/STOL concept, the Harrier remains unique in the world. The Soviet Yakovlev Yak-36MP, which was patterned after the original Kestrel concept, is in service with the Soviet Navy. In the Yak-36MP's current form, however, it is considered nowhere near as versatile or capable as the Harrier. By the mid-1990s, there will almost certainly be new and superior V/STOL aircraft that will come on the scene. But in the meantime, when a Marine ground commander needs air support and the Marine air commander says "jump," there will be only one jump jet.

McDONNELL DOUGLAS AV-8B HARRIER

Wingspan:	30 ft. 3½ in.
Length:	42 ft. 10 in.
Height:	11 ft. 3½ in.
Engine:	one Rolls-Royce F402-RR-402 turbojet
Engine thrust (lbs.):	21,500
Gross weight (lbs.):	18,450
Operating altitude (ft.):	51,000
Top speed (mph):	662
Maximum range (miles):	1,550

Two Marine Corps Harriers out of Yuma, Arizona, each lug four 500-pound Mark 82 bombs and a pair of air-to-air Sidewinder missiles.

Harriers peel away from a KC-130 tanker to unload their ordnance on the Yuma range.

Left: The Harrier's huge Rolls-Royce Pegasus engine, with its 21,500 pounds of thrust, requires large air intakes. Note the odd four-point landing gear. *Above, top:* Variable-thrust nozzles, two on each side of the fuselage, are the key to the Harrier's unique capabilities. *Above, bottom:* Marine Harrier driver Capt. Glenn "Birdman" Pheasant awaits the signal to light the wick.

153

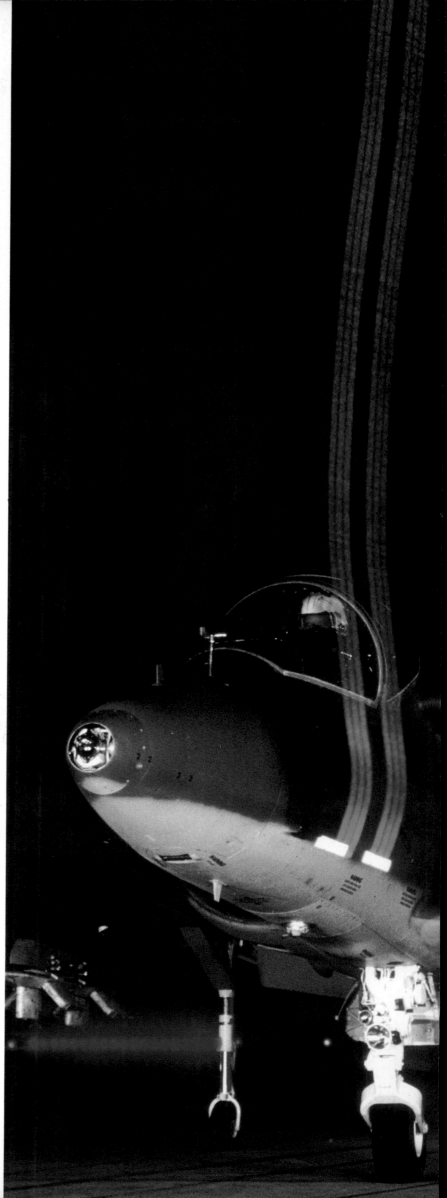

Above: The cockpit of the AV-8B Harrier. *Right:* A Harrier "drops in" at Yuma after a night bombing mission. Harrier pilots practice vertical landings on a regular basis.

A Harrier in a Yuma sunset.

A-7
CORSAIR II

The A-7's gaping mouth makes it look like a startled dwarf, but appearances are deceiving. The A-7 takes its name from a far more graceful ancestor, and the A-7's overall appearance is from an older cousin. The ancestor was the great Vought F4U Corsair, a gull-winged World War II fighter, which served with Marine Corps units in the South Pacific and on U.S. Navy carriers in the latter part of the war (Pappy Boyington's infamous "Black Sheep" squadron flew Corsairs). In the Korean War, the Corsair became a fighter-bomber, which is how the name was passed down.

The Corsair II's older cousin was the Vought F8U (F-8 after 1962) Crusader that served as one of the Navy's top carrier fighters before and during the Vietnam War. Aside from the F-4 Phantom II, Crusaders claimed more enemy MiGs in Vietnam than any other American aircraft.

The Corsair II also served in Vietnam, having first flown in 1965. The idea behind the Corsair II was to build a light attack plane to complement the Navy's A-4. Vought, which had merged with Ling-Temco in 1961, won the contract by suggesting a compact, scaled-down aircraft based on the F-8. Even as A-7 deliveries to the Navy were getting under way, the Air Force was discovering that it had a need for attack aircraft in Vietnam that could not be fully met by fighter-bombers. The Air Force then decided to join the Navy program and acquire A-7s for itself.

The first Corsair II mission in Vietnam was flown by Navy A-7As off the carrier USS *Ranger* in December 1967, and the last was actually the final American combat mission of the war, flown by Air Force A-7Ds against targets in Cambodia on August 15, 1973. The A-7 proved to be a very reliable, stable performer. The Air Force, for example, flew 12,928 Corsair II missions in Southeast Asia—including many against targets in heavily defended North Vietnam—with only four losses!

Today, Corsair IIs remain the principal component in U.S. Navy carrier-based light attack squadrons, having replaced A-4s. On the Air Force side, A-7s are used only by the Air National Guard, but they equip more Guard units than any other combat aircraft. Overseas, both Greece and Portugal use A-7s.

The Corsair II is a single-place aircraft, although 60 of them have been converted to two-place combat-capable trainers that could be used in the attack role in an emergency. The aircraft's armament consists of nearly eight tons of bombs, and AGM-65 Maverick and AGM-88 HARM air-to-ground missiles or AIM-9 Sidewinder air-to-air missiles for self-defense. For general all-around use, Corsair IIs carry a 20-millimeter cannon. Although the A-7s are constantly being updated as a matter of course, LTV has proposed several all new aircraft based on the Corsair II. These would go into production if there were customer interest and include the Corsair III and a supersonic variant called Strikefighter. Despite the Corsair II's age, the durability of the A-7 fleet, amply demonstrated in Vietnam, will almost certainly make it a valuable asset for years to come.

LTV (LING-TEMCO-VOUGHT) A-7E CORSAIR II

Wingspan:	38 ft. 9 in.
Length:	46 ft. 1½ in.
Height:	16 ft. ¾ in.
Engine:	one Allison TF41-A-2 turbofan
Engine thrust (lbs.):	15,000
Maximum T-O weight (lbs.):	42,000
Operating altitude (ft.):	37,910
Cruising speed (mph):	470
Top speed (mph):	691
Maximum range (miles):	2,861

Right: **An A-7, loaded with 500-pound Mark 82 iron bombs, rolls in over its target on the Fallon, Nevada, range.**

Left: A Corsair fires a 5-inch ZUNI air-to-ground rocket. *Above*: The A-7 is no fighter, but it often carries Sidewinders on fuselage rails for defense following a ground attack.

Above: An Air Guard A-7K gasses up from a KC-135 while a boom operator, getting a rare familiarization ride in the back seat, watches the operation from the other end. *Right:* A quartet of two-seat A-7Ks, based with the Arizona Air National Guard training wing at Tucson, Arizona.

The deck director positions a Corsair on the bow catapult of the USS *Constellation*. The wings will be unfolded immediately before catapult hook-up to the nose gear.

A-10 THUNDERBOLT II

Nobody calls the Fairchild Republic A-10 the "Thunderbolt." Even its friends call it the "Warthog." The idea for the A-10—when it was still on the drawing boards—was for it to take the name of the famous Republic P-47 Thunderbolt, a World War II fighter that had become renowned as a fighter-bomber. But the A-10 did not turn out to be a graceful, proud-looking bird like the P-47 had been.

The A-10 can unleash a withering thunderbolt of destructive power, and this is the A-10's reason for being. From World War II until the Vietnam War, the U.S. Air Force had spent a great deal of time and money on fighters and bombers and almost nothing on the ground attack/close air support role that it was obliged to provide for the Army. In Vietnam, the Air Force ended up using a combination of World War II planes, converted trainers, fighter-bombers, and borrowed Navy types for the job. Thus, it became clear that a warplane dedicated solely to the job of close air support was a vital necessity, especially as the Air Force reevaluated its obligations to the Army in light of its Vietnam experience.

In 1972, the Air Force considered both the Northrop A-9 and the Fairchild Republic A-10, and chose to put the A-10 into full-scale squadron service. The first A-10 unit became operational in 1977, and the last of 713 Warthogs was delivered to the Air Force in 1984.

Today, Warthogs are in service with the Tactical Air Command and with reserve units in the continental United States, as well as with Air Force units in Korea and Alaska. The largest concentration of A-10s, however, is in western Europe, where they would be an integral part of blunting any Warsaw Pact invasion. In the event of a total war in Europe, the task of the Warthog drivers would be monumental because the scale of the enemy attack would be nearly overwhelming. Under these circumstances, A-10 pilots would find themselves literally surrounded by potential targets.

In such an environment, an attack aircraft would have to have the capacity to destroy anything in its path and to withstand the ground fire hurled at it. In terms of the latter characteristic, the Warthog is one of the "hardest" aircraft flying. The pilot sits in a titanium-armor "bathtub" that can withstand incoming rounds from 23-millimeter cannons. Control lines are duplicated and stretched through widely separate parts of the aircraft, so that if one is shot out another can take over. The heavily armored 'Hog has its engines located high and to the rear, to give them maximum shielding from ground-launched heat-seeking missiles. The A-10 is even designed to fly home with one of its engines, or half its tail, blown completely off.

The offensive characteristics of the Warthog are equally impressive and have earned it the additional nickname of "tank-buster." The centerpiece of the A-10's suite of armaments is the huge GAU-8 Avenger 30-millimeter rotary cannon. The largest forward-firing aerial cannon in the Air Force, the seven-barreled Avenger packs nearly 1,200 rounds of extra-long (six-inch), extra-potent, high-velocity slugs with depleted uranium tips. No longer radioactive, the uranium is used because it is heavier than lead or steel and thus will slam its way through a thicker slab of armor plate. The Avenger is, by itself, capable of taking out an enemy battle tank.

In addition to its Avenger, the A-10 can carry eight tons of just about any type of air-to-ground munitions in the Air Force. Electronic countermeasures equipment can also be carried on the A-10's eight underwing pylons, as can AIM-9 Sidewinders.

FAIRCHILD REPUBLIC A-10A THUNDERBOLT II	
Wingspan:	57 ft. 6 in.
Length:	53 ft. 4 in.
Height:	14 ft. 8 in.
Engines:	two General Electric TF34-GE-100 turbofans
Engine thrust (lbs.):	9,065
Maximum T-O weight (lbs.):	50,000
Operating altitude (ft.):	37,800
Cruising speed (mph):	387
Top speed (mph):	439
Maximum range (miles):	2,454

Right: **An Air Force Reserve A-10 Warthog unloads a pair of Mark 82 500-pound bombs. Inflatable retarders are used for low-level drops to pull the bombs away and to the rear of the jet.**

A pair of A-10 Warthogs, slinging tiny practice bombs, pose for the photographer who sits in the co-pilot's seat of KC-135 tanker.

Above: A Warthog driver checks his six (his aft) for his trailing wingman. The fish-eye lens makes the wings appear swept; in fact, the A-10 has long, straight wings that give it amazing snap-turn capabilities at low speeds. *Right:* Above the Mississippi range, a 'Hog starts to roll in over its target. Blue bombs are inert practice dummies.

Left: The A-10's big turbofans are mounted high and far apart to ensure that one engine, if damaged and disintegrating, won't hurl junk into the other. *Above:* A 'Hog driver lets loose with the awesome 30-millimeter antitank cannon in the A-10's nose.

Above: The A-10 cockpit is a model of simplicity compared with most modern attack jets. The twin yellow handles fire the pilot's ejection seat. *Right:* A-10s out of Myrtle Beach AFB, South Carolina, fire up at Nellis AFB in Las Vegas.

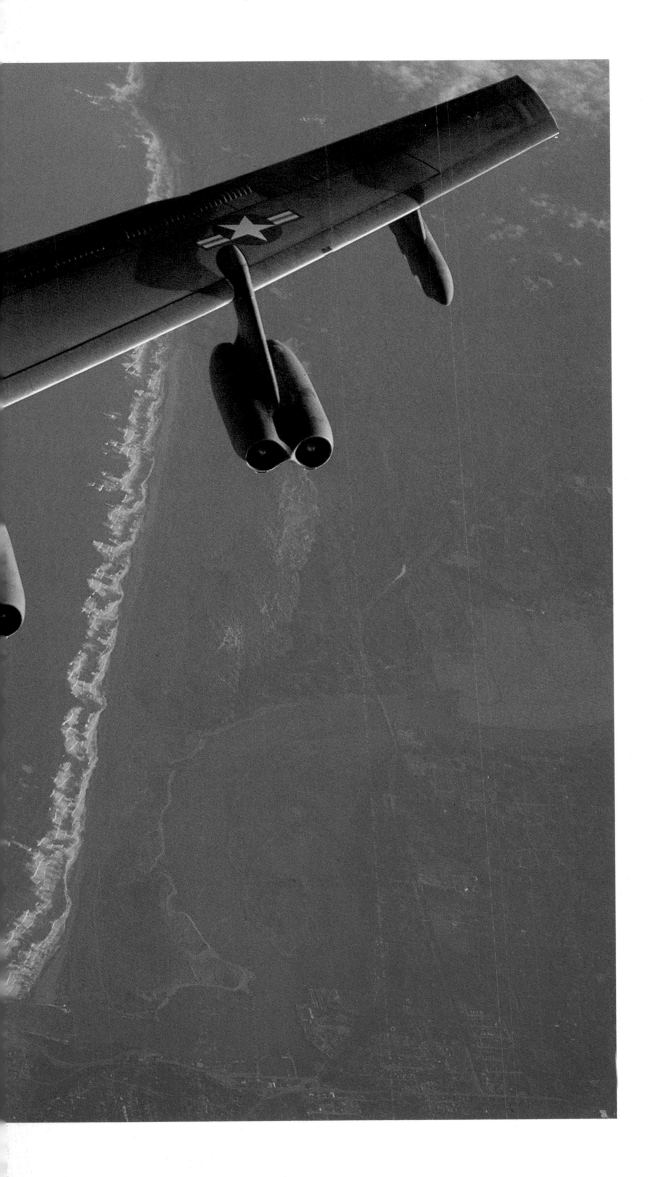

BOMBERS

A B-52H over the Oregon coast.

177

In World War II they lumbered across the sky, creating an "aluminum overcast" that blotted out the sun over Germany and Japan. They played a pivotal role in bringing Allied retribution to the front doors of the Axis nations.

Bombers may be fewer and farther between now than they were in the vast armadas of World War II, but the role of bombers today is the same as it was then: to destroy the enemy's will to wage war. Fighters may sweep the sky of enemy warplanes and secure the skyways, but bombers win wars.

Bombers are incredibly expensive machines, running into hundreds of millions of dollars, and it is hard to justify such an expense if you aren't planning a war. On the other hand, war often seeks out just those people who aren't planning wars. It happened at Pearl Harbor on December 7, 1941, and it could happen tomorrow. Anywhere. The attack on Pearl Harbor and the anguish of World War II had a lot to do with the creation of the U.S. Air Force's Strategic Air Command (SAC). SAC was born in 1946—an outgrowth of the huge bomber force that was built up during the Second World War—and it has been the biggest strategic bomber force in the West ever since. Until the mid-1960s it was the largest in the world, but the Soviet Air Force Long Range Aviation has become at least half-again larger since that time.

Strategic bombers have always been designed around the principle of getting to the target, hitting it, and getting home to fly again. What was true of B-17s in 1942 is true of B-1Bs today. The technology of accomplishing this mission has changed, but that's a function of the changing nature of enemy defenses. The more sophisticated the enemy radar gets, the more sophisticated the electronic countermeasures must be. It's as simple as that.

The bombs, too, have changed. They had changed a lot during World War II, too. The bombers of that era carried around eight tons of conventional bombs, but when the *Enola Gay* went to Hiroshima in August 1945, a single bomb had several thousand times the destructive force of a whole bomber-load of bombs.

Nuclear weapons changed everything. They made war so unthinkable that they've actually acted to prevent a third world war in the decades following 1945. SAC was born with the advent of nuclear weapons, and it was also the force that carried the threat that kept the Soviet Bear at bay during all those years. SAC kept the Cold War cold.

The evolution of bombers during this era was very similar to that of the parallel series of fighters; both bombers and fighters got faster and faster. The B-47 and B-52, of 1947 and 1951 respectively, were faster than anything seen during World War II, but they were still subsonic. The B-58, which first flew in 1956, was the world's first supersonic bomber. The XB-70, which first flew eight years later, could cruise at *three* times the speed of sound. By 1970, however, only the B-52 remained, and it is still in service today.

In Vietnam, SAC and the Air Force learned that there was still a call for conventional bombing, and this realization played a key role in the design of today's B-1B. This means that today's American bomber force is more versatile—far better equipped for its conventional as well as nuclear missions.

What, then, is the nature of this force? In mid-1988, it consisted of more than 250 B-52G and B-52H heavy bombers, a quarter-century-old and aging; 99 B-1Bs, most of which were less than two years old; and 60 15-year-old FB-111s, the SAC version of the F-111 Aardvark. At the same time, the first of the new B-2 "Stealth" bombers was still a few years from being operational.

In terms of armament, the longest legs of the SAC bomber force are the AGM-86 Air Launched Cruise Missiles (ALCM), 21-foot-long pilotless airplanes each with a nuclear business end that can be dropped by a bomber 1,500 miles from its target. Once dropped, the ALCM's jet engine is started and it begins a very low-level penetration of enemy territory. Like an airplane, the ALCM is very maneuverable. Its robot memory is programmed with the route of its predetermined target. It knows where to turn to avoid a hill here, and where it can dive into a canyon to avoid radar detection there. It can be very hard to catch because it flies so low that it gets caught in "ground clutter" on enemy radar. It can use hills, canyons, and even power lines as "blinds" to shield itself. A bomber that uses the ALCM can hit a number of targets on one mission and turn back for home 1,500 miles short of reaching any of them. More than 100 B-52s have been modified to carry a dozen ALCMs each, and the B-1B can also carry a dozen ALCMs externally, as well as another eight inside its weapons bay on a rotary launcher.

Other bomber weapons include, of course, bombs. For a conventional mission, B-52s, B-1Bs, and FB-111s can carry an assortment of quarter- and half-ton unguided "gravity," or "iron," bombs, or GBU-series guided "glide" bombs (also known as "smart bombs"). Also available are 14-foot AQM-69 Short Range Attack Missiles. SRAMs are the original "stand-off" weapon. Like the ALCM, the pilot can release SRAMs before he is over a target to avoid getting nailed by anti-aircraft artillery.

The kilotonnage capacity of SAC's bomber fleet is staggering. While the Intercontinental Ballistic Missiles (ICBMs) of the Soviet Union and the United States have become the focal point in discussions about nuclear war and nuclear weaponry, the capabilities of both sides' bombers are often tossed off as "obsolete." Billions have been spent on the respective "Star Wars" defense systems (the Soviets have one as well), but bombers will always be more versatile and harder to catch than ICBMs, even after such grandiose projects are deployed. A B-1B can scramble out of a base on the edge of the South Dakota Badlands at 4:00 a.m., be at the North Pole by mid-morning, and be able to take out at least a dozen major military or industrial targets in the Soviet Union by noon. An ICBM can move a lot faster, but since the Soviets know where the launch sites are, ICBMs are easier to track and predict. A bomber over the North Pole is a lot more unpredictable. The pilot can, of course, be called off if the alert is a false alarm (an ICBM cannot); the pilot can make a radical turn in any direction (an ICBM cannot); and once within range, the pilot can blanket an area 3,000 miles across with ALCMs. Even with multiple warheads, an ICBM couldn't provide such versatility.

Combining such firepower and versatility into a hard-to-track, low-flying aircraft maneuvered by the mind and hand of a human being makes the modern strategic bomber a very powerful weapon indeed.

The design of the air intakes on the earlier B-1A increased the size of the bomber's radar cross section.

B-52 STRATOFORTRESS

In the pantheon of the world's truly great warplanes, only the venerable (it's earned the adjective) B-52 has survived in front-line service long enough to have been used by *three* generations of pilots. There are crew members aboard Boeing B-52s today whose grandfathers flew B-52s!

It is a remarkable testament to a plane that was really only meant to last a half dozen years (a decade at the most). Boeing had built the B-17 Flying Fortress and the B-29 Superfortress, two of the most important (if not *the* two most important) warplanes of World War II. Boeing also built the B-47 Stratojet, the first all-jet, swept-wing bomber to go into service with the U.S. Air Force after the war. Development of the plane that would become the B-52 began in the late 1940s, with the idea of building an all-jet swept-wing bomber with a conventional as well as a nuclear-bomb capacity that had a truly *intercontinental* range. The Convair B-36, the largest bomber in history, had the intercontinental range but it was slow and cumbersome, a straight-winged behemoth that had been designed during World War II. For Boeing, the idea was to develop something entirely new that would break new ground and that would remain in the arsenal until at least the 1960s. Little did anyone realize in 1948 that the B-52 would still be around in the 1990s.

The B-52 made its first flight in 1951 and entered service with the U.S. Air Force's Strategic Air Command (SAC) in 1954, a year after the Soviet Union exploded its first hydrogen bomb. Like that of SAC itself, the principal job of the B-52 in the 1950s—as in the 1980s—was to deter nuclear aggression against the United States by demonstrating the capacity and readiness to deliver an equal counterblow against the aggressor. They were eight-engined giants that were described at the time as "the most formidable expression of air power in the history of military aviation."

Aside from a handful of B-52s assigned to the Air Force Systems Command for various testing purposes, all of the 744 Stratofortresses that Boeing built between 1951 and 1963 spent their entire careers in service with SAC. There were two prototypes, 447 of the characteristic tall-tailed B-52A through B-52F types, 193 low-tailed B-52Gs, and 102 low-tailed B-52H models that were powered by eight turbofan (rather than turbojet) engines. The B-52H turbofans deliver an aggregate of 110,000 pounds of thrust, versus 80,000 pounds of thrust delivered by the eight turbojets of the B-52D.

In 1957, as a demonstration of their intercontinental capabilities, three B-52s were flown (with aerial refuelings en route) nonstop 24,325 miles *around the world.* Five years later, a B-52H flew 12,532 miles nonstop without refueling, setting a distance record that stood until the flight of the *Voyager* a quarter-century later. It was this type of operational capability that gave the B-52 a much deserved reputation for durability and tenacity.

After a decade of service in a nuclear-deterrent capacity only, SAC B-52s were detailed to Vietnam in 1965 for the Operation Arc Light carpet-bombing raids on suspected Viet Cong strongholds. In 1972, SAC B-52s based in Guam and Thailand conducted an 11-day series of strategic bombing missions against Hanoi (during Operation Linebacker II) that largely destroyed North Vietnam's war-making capacity. This paved the way for a cease-fire after nearly a decade of intense U.S. involvement in the war in Southeast Asia.

Several times before Vietnam, and several times since, the Air Force has attempted to replace the B-52. These attempts have ranged from complex feasibility

(continued on p. 182)

Right: A B-52 refuels from a KC-135 tanker over the Oregon coast.

(continued from p. 180)

studies to full-scale development and deployment of such strategic bombers as the B-58 and the B-70. It was not until the B-1B became operational in 1985 (30 years after the B-52) that SAC has had a heavy strategic bomber in service that is likely to outlive the B-52.

Since 1984, only the low-tailed B-52G and B-52H models have remained in service, and there is every indication that the B-52H (if not both) will remain until the mid-1990s or beyond.

Known familiarly as the "Big Ugly Fat Fellow (BUFF)," the B-52 of today is a far different airplane from a pilot's-eye view than the B-52 of three generations ago. The eight throttle levers are still there—and it's the only cockpit in the world where you'll see *eight*—but many other details have changed. Both the pilot's and copilot's station have been transformed by green electro-optical viewing system (EVS) screens that provide visual data from the forward-looking infrared sensor (FLIR), and low-light television (LLTV) cameras that protrude from the chin of today's BUFF. The FLIR sensors provide the pilot with an image of daylight clarity even during periods of low visibility due to fog and storms, while the LLTV camera provides a clear image even during starlight. Together, they permit operations during all visibility conditions. These systems, combined with advanced terrain-avoidance radar, permit low-level B-52 missions under virtually any conditions.

Once a high-altitude strategic bomber in the spirit of its World War II Boeing ancestors, the B-52 of today is capable of a multitude of missions. The newly acquired low-level capability permits extremely long-range penetration beneath enemy radar, while the same long-range capability that made the B-52 a wonder in the 1950s permits today's BUFF to fly cruise or Harpoon missile missions thousands of miles from its base.

The B-52 is a venerable warhorse, but it's hardly ready to be put out to pasture.

BOEING B-52H STRATOFORTRESS	
Wingspan:	185 ft.
Length:	160 ft. 11 in.
Height:	40 ft. 8 in.
Engines:	eight Pratt & Whitney TF33-P-3 turbofans
Engine thrust (lbs.):	13,750
Maximum T-O weight (lbs.):	488,000
Operating altitude (ft.):	55,000
Cruising speed (mph):	509
Top speed (mph):	595
Maximum range (miles):	10,145

This shot of a fat and happy BUFF was taken from the tanker that refueled it.

Left: The B-52's wings sag when filled with fuel, hence the small outrigger "training wheels" at the wingtips.
Above, top: A trio of Air Launched Cruise Missiles (ALCMs) is installed on the wing pylon of a B-52 at Griffiss AFB, New York.
Above, bottom: The ancient B-52 requires tremendous amounts of expensive maintenance.

Left: The B-52 spews out horrifying amounts of exhaust. *Above, top:* The B-52 carries .50-caliber machine guns. *Above, center:* The B-52's windowless "mushroom factory." *Above, bottom:* Television and infrared sensors have been installed on this B-52H.

F-111/FB-111 AARDVARK

There have been a lot of airplanes called "ugly ducklings," but there has been only one Aardvark. It was the plane that nobody wanted, the plane that cost too much, and the plane that didn't work. It was the plane that was the brainchild of a man who disliked airplanes and one of the unfortunates to earn the epithet "widowmaker." It was born as a fighter, yet lived its whole life as a bomber. It was the Aardvark.

To the North Vietnamese in 1972, however, it became "whispering death," and to Muammar Qaddafi in 1986 it was a terrible nightmare.

Its story began in the mid-1960s, when the Defense Department under Secretary Robert McNamara conceived the idea for a tactical fighter-bomber that could be used by both the Air Force and the Navy. Proposals for an experimental prototype of such an airplane, designated TFX (for tactical fighter, experimental), were submitted by Boeing and General Dynamics. General Dynamics was awarded the contract to build the airplane. The prototype made its first flight in December 1964, and plans were laid to begin producing an F-111A for the Air Force and an F-111B for the Navy. However, McNamara's dream of versatility was elusive. The more the project evolved, the more disparate the requirements of the two services became. The more the design was changed to please one service, the less it matched the needs of the other.

In 1968, the Navy dropped out of the project, and the Air Force went ahead alone with 141 F-111As, while Australia ordered 24 F-111Cs. These were followed over the years by 296 F-111D, E, and F aircraft (with improved systems) that came off the assembly line through 1976 and that were delivered into fighter-bomber service with the U.S. Air Force's Tactical Air Command (TAC). The Strategic Air Command (SAC), meanwhile, acquired 76 of them to use as medium bombers under the designation FB-111. It was a strange evolution for the plane once known as TFX.

When the F-111 first went into combat in Vietnam in 1967, the results were disastrous. There were structural defects traceable to years of fiddling with the design. There were also serious problems with the then-experimental terrain-following radar that was supposed to permit extremely low-level bombing missions deep in North Vietnam. The F-111 was withdrawn, but when it was reintroduced in 1972, its story had changed completely.

Instead of uncertain death for American crew members, it was "whispering death" for the enemy. The F-111s came in so fast and so low that the first sound enemy troops heard was that of exploding bombs.

Having proved itself in the last full year of American involvement in Southeast Asia, the F-111 went on to become the airplane of choice for TAC units specified to perform long-range, deep-interdiction attacks against targets within enemy territory. Gradually, the ugly airplane with the turned-up nose won the hearts of its aircrews and won it the nickname "Aardvark." A decade came and went, and the 'Varks remained on duty, preparing for potential bombing missions should the need arise. With air bases of Warsaw Pact forces seen as a likely target in the event of a major European conflict, a wing of F-111s was stationed in England just to be ready, and there they waited.

By the spring of 1986, the prospective threat to the security of Americans in the world had shifted from the potential of a war with the Soviet Union to the bloody reality of vicious terrorism. The job of striking the terrorist nerve center in Muammar Qaddafi's capital at Tripoli fell to the U.S. Air Force F-111s based in Britain. Eighteen 'Varks made the 5,750-mile bomb run on April 15, 1986 (with the support of U.S. Air Force aerial refueling planes), and succeeded in dropping more than 70 tons of unguided and laser-guided bombs on Qaddafi's terrorist enclave.

With a Mach 2 speed, the Aardvark is faster than other American bombers, a characteristic that, when combined with a range that exceeds that of American fighters, makes it a unique and valuable airplane. Its bomberlike cockpit features side-by-side seating for the pilot and weapons systems operator. This is a characteristic that would have been cumbersome in a fighter, where a clear, unobstructed view for the pilot is essential, but a necessity in a bomber, where the need for the two crew members to work together is essential.

(continued on p. 191)

Right: SAC operates FB-111 'Varks, long-range variants with greater internal fuel capacity.

(continued from p. 188)

The F-111 can be configured to carry 12 tons of bombs and missiles of various types and in various combinations. The FB-111, meanwhile, is rather like a miniature B-52, with a 16-ton nuclear or conventional bomb load. The FB-111 can trade five of those tons for four AGM-69 Short Range Attack Missiles. These weapons are carried on swiveling pylons located beneath the variable-geometry wings, the sweep of which—like the wings of the F-14 and B-1B—is designed so that it can be changed in flight from nearly straight for a slow, level cruise to a virtual delta configuration for a high-speed dash.

GENERAL DYNAMICS F-111F

Wingspan (unswept):	63 ft.
Wingspan (swept):	32 ft.
Length:	73 ft. 6 in.
Height:	17 ft.
Engines:	two Pratt & Whitney JF30-P-100 turbofans
Engine thrust (lbs.):	25,100
Gross weight (lbs.):	95,333
Operating altitude (ft.):	57,900
Cruising speed (mph):	498
Top speed (mph):	1,453
Maximum range (miles):	3,378

The FB-111 is operated by SAC as a small strategic bomber.

Above: An F-111 pilot performs preflight checks prior to a tactical hop in Europe. *Right:* An F-111F peels away from his wingman over the North Sea. The variable-sweep wings are in the forward position.

The boom operator's view of an F-111 cockpit while refueling.

Although less than a beautiful bird, this F-111 strikes an elegant pose over a wintry English sky.

Despite its great bulk and weight, the F-111 is enormously fast. It is capable of exceeding Mach 1 at sea level with considerable ease.

It took the Rockwell International B-1 a long time, but if it can survive the politicians' attempts to kill it, it should be able to survive anything.

The idea behind the B-1 is not new. The B-1 concept actually dates back to the idea of developing an eventual successor to the B-52, and *that* dates back to the deployment of the B-52 in the mid-1950s. The B-58 and B-70 came and went as potential successors, and by 1962, the Air Force had undertaken the Advanced Manned Strategic Aircraft (AMSA) program, which was shorthand for a new strategic bomber. The emphasis on "manned" was to distinguish the system from the unmanned ballistic missiles, of which Defense Secretary Robert McNamara was so fond.

The huge Mach 3 XB-70 was perceived as being too much airplane for too much money, so AMSA would have to be a lesser airplane. When the contract was finally issued in 1970, it went to the North American Division of Rockwell International, which had, as North American Aviation, developed the XB-70. Built under the designation B-1, the first of the new strategic bombers made its maiden flight in December 1974. Three of the billion-dollar bombers had been built by 1977 when President Jimmy Carter made good on a campaign promise and canceled the program, reducing it from an operational to a flight-test only program. Four years later, however, the need to find a suitable replacement for the B-52 was more critical than ever. In 1981 President Ronald Reagan revived the program under the designation B-1B.

The program called for using two B-1A aircraft for flight-testing a host of new systems and for building 100 brand-new operational B-1B aircraft, which not only would incorporate these new systems but would feature many new design elements. The latter would include redesigned engine air intakes that would help reduce the radar profile of the B-1A (which was already just one-tenth that of a B-52) by 90 percent in the B-1B. This meant that the B-1B, which was 147 feet long compared with a 162-foot B-52, would appear on radar as only being *20 inches long* compared with a B-52! Because of its radar profile, a B-1B can, theoretically, penetrate enemy airspace with a 99 times better chance of getting through a radar net than a B-52. The redesigned intakes cut the speed of the B-1B to just over Mach 1, compared with double that for the B-1A, but this is still half again faster than the B-52.

The first B-1B rolled out of the factory in September 1984 and made its initial flight the following month. The first full B-1B squadron became operational with the U.S. Air Force Strategic Air Command (SAC) in October 1986, and the one hundredth and last B-1B was completed—under budget and ahead of schedule—in April, 1988.

The B-1B is designed to do what the B-52 can do and more. Theoretically, it has the same range, but precise figures are classified. The bomb load of the B-1B is actually larger than that of the B-52, despite the B-1B's smaller size. This translates to roughly half again more bomb tonnage and the internal capacity to carry 24 AGM-69 Short Range Attack Missiles (compared with 20 in a B-52H), plus another 14 on external racks under the fuselage. The B-1B is configured with a unique rotary launcher that can accommodate eight Air Launched Cruise Missiles (ALCM) in the internal weapons bay and another 14 outside. The B-52H, meanwhile, can carry a dozen ALCMs on external racks, while only some Stratofortresses are configured to carry eight ALCMs internally.

The specifications make the B-1B look like a formidable bomber on paper, the view from the cockpit makes the plane seem like a fighter. It can accelerate fast, turn quickly, and on more than one occasion, it has climbed out of a low-level, Mach 0.9 flight so rapidly that accompanying fighters were left in the dust, their pilots gawking in disbelief. The B-52 was designed for stately soaring at high altitudes and later modified for low-level missions. The B-1B, however, was *designed* for the low-level environment and that makes it an airplane that is very much at home snapping fast turns around jagged mountains and banking into 45-degree turns.

A major difference between the cockpits of the two planes is that while the B-52 was designed with an airliner-type yoke, the B-1B cockpit was designed with a stick. It's much less cumbersome and makes the pilot feel like he's flying a fighter.

Like a fighter, the B-1B is a pilot's airplane. Many of the pilots who fly it today came to the plane from other big, multi-engine airplanes, like the B-52. These pilots found the B-1B's agility surprising and came to love it. It is a remarkable airplane. It even surprised the politicians who had opposed it.

Conversely, the *elimination* of surprise is very much what the B-1B, like the B-52, is all about. The job of preventing a nuclear first strike against the United States falls to SAC and its bombers, and the B-1B will do its part until the turn of the century, and beyond.

(continued on p. 200)

Right: Air-conditioning "spaghetti" cools on-board electronics during pre-start checks.

(continued from p. 198)

ROCKWELL INTERNATIONAL B-1B

Wingspan (unswept):	136 ft. 8½ in.
Wingspan (swept):	78 ft. 2½ in.
Length:	147 ft.
Height:	34 ft.
Engines:	four General Electric F101-GE-102 turbofans
Engine thrust (lbs.):	30,000
Maximum T-O weight (lbs.):	477,000
Operating altitude (ft.):	60,000
Top speed (mph):	Mach 1.25
Maximum range (miles):	7,455

A B-1B undergoing final flight testing at Edwards AFB, California.

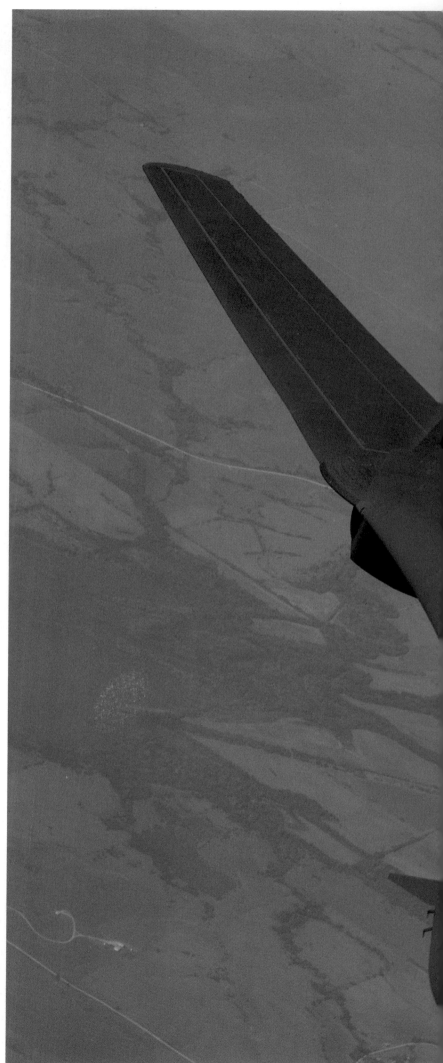

Above: A B-1B bomber approaches its tanker over central Kansas. Note the open fuel port in front of the windshield. The white markings facilitate refueling in limited light. *Right:* A B-1B out of McConnell AFB, Kansas.

203

A prototype B-1A under construction at the Palmdale, California, plant of Rockwell International.

A B-1A on a test flight out of Edwards AFB, California.

Early B-1As, while under-
going testing at Edwards
AFB, were painted white
and fitted with instrument-
filled nose probes.

P-3
ORION

If the P-3 is a bomber, why does it have a "P" instead of a "B" in the designation? In actual fact, the "P" for "Patrol" in U.S. Navy nomenclature dates back to the "patrol bombers" that the Navy flew in large numbers during World War II and earlier. In those days, most of the patrol bombers were seaplanes, but a great many were land-based bombers that were identical to, or very like, the B-24s and B-25s that the USAAF (now U.S. Air Force) was flying. It's worth mentioning that there have been unofficial proposals lately calling for the Air Force to acquire Orions under the B-3 designation.

Lockheed has been building land-based patrol bombers for the Navy since before World War II. Since the war, the entire history of such planes is summarized by the Lockheed P2V (P-2 after 1962) Neptune and the Lockheed P3V (P-3 after 1962) Orion.

The role of the Navy's patrol bombers is simply to patrol vast areas of ocean and to bomb anything—whether it be a surface ship or submarine—that constitutes a threat to American territory or American ships. The Neptune was in service from 1946 until the late 1970s, when it was gradually phased out. The Orion (which was based on the design of the Electra airliner) entered service in 1962 and, in one form or another, will probably remain in service until the turn of the century.

Well over 600 Orions have been built. Most of them are the P-3C type, which was first introduced in 1970. A majority of deliveries have been to the U.S. Navy, but other user nations include Australia, New Zealand, Norway, Iran, Japan, and the Netherlands. Canada ordered 18 Orions, which it refers to as "CP-140 Auroras."

The role of a patrol bomber is hardly a glamorous one for P-3 crews, who must survey thousands of square miles of open sea on 12-hour patrols. The patrols' duration matches or exceeds that flown by the crews of U.S. Air Force B-52s. Frequently, the Orion's crew will track targets, such as submarines, that it can't even see. Big Soviet nuclear subs routinely patrol the United States coastline just outside American territorial waters—closer than many Americans would like to think. With equal routine, the P-3s are out there, dropping sonar buoys to monitor the position of the known submarines, and keeping a lookout for other yet unseen threats, which will, in turn, be monitored by the P-3s on the next shift.

If a submarine warship did, in fact, become a hostile threat, the Orion crews would be ready to open their bomb bays and drop one-ton or half-ton mines, or Mark 46 torpedoes, that would seek out and destroy the threatening vessel. As with any weapon that serves in a deterrent role, just having the P-3s on station, day after day, helps to keep would-be aggressors *at* bay, and *out* of the bays of the American coastline.

LOCKHEED P-3C ORION	
Wingspan:	99 ft. 8 in.
Length:	116 ft. 10 in.
Height:	33 ft. 8½ in.
Engines:	four Allison T56-A-14 turboprops
Engine (hp):	4,910
Maximum T-O weight (lbs.):	135,000
Operating altitude (ft.):	28,300
Cruising speed (mph):	378
Top speed (mph):	473
Maximum range (miles):	4,766

Right: The Lockheed P-3, a military version of the popular 1950s commercial airliner Electra, is the Navy's principal land-based anti-submarine warfare (ASW) asset.

The Orion's forward bomb bay can be loaded with a variety of antisubmarine torpedoes and other lethal ordnance.

A Naval Reserve Orion, based at NAS Moffett Field, California, makes an ID pass over an incoming merchantman.

The P-3 is America's fastest turboprop plane, with a top speed well over 400 mph.

P-3 missions are long and tedious, often exceeding eight hours. The tail extension is a MAD (Metal Anomaly Detection) capable of sensing the metallic mass of a submarine below the surface.

"STEALTH"

It is perhaps the most well-known "secret" aircraft to enter the American arsenal since World War II. When the B-2 program was first disclosed in 1980, all that was known was that the Air Force was developing a bomber that would incorporate a mysterious technology called "stealth," which could render the aircraft invisible to radar. For eight years, no details of the plane—not even its *shape*—were officially announced. Finally, in late 1988, the B-2 was unveiled to the press.

Stealth technology is, in fact, a whole basket of techniques, used together, that are not terribly mysterious. But the idea of combining the whole basket into one aircraft and making that the guiding factor in the plane's design really wasn't considered until the 1970s. By then, advances in nonmetallic structural materials made new techniques possible; advances in radar and radar-guided anti-aircraft missile technology made it necessary.

To create an airplane that is invisible to radar, a design team would first have to examine the nature of radar. Radar doesn't perceive size, only contour, shape, and surfaces. A glossy, light-colored surface reflects light and also reflects radar back to its receiver, so the design-

ers would paint the airplane with a dark, flat, radar-absorbing paint. Metallic surfaces also reflect radar, so the use of such a nonmetallic plastic material as Kevlar would go a long way toward reducing radar detectability.

Jet engines, especially when they are hanging under a wing on pylons, are very easy for radar to spot, so the designers would conceal them entirely within the wing or fuselage. Even the difference between the way the engine turbine blades were concealed on the B-1B reduced its radar visibility by up to 90 percent, compared with the B-1A. (It is also painted a very dark camouflage color.)

Finally, hard edges and sharp angles are always radar visible, so every effort would be made to smooth out corners and edges. Even the B-1A had only 10 percent of the cross section of the B-52 because its engines partially blended into the fuselage and there was a smoother contour between the fuselage and wings.

The confluence of wing and fuselage and the multitude of sharp and even right angles in an airplane's tail would present a final and unique challenge to the stealth designers, yet one that could easily be solved just by getting rid of it all. An airplane doesn't need a fuselage to

fly, it only needs a wing, so you can simply make the wing thicker (radar doesn't discern size, only contour) and put the crew, the engines, and the weapons inside.

The precedent for flying wings goes back to the experiments of Jack Northrop's design team in the 1940s. In fact, Northrop built two types of flying wing strategic bombers—the YB-35 and YB-49—for the U.S. Air Force in the early 1950s; each had a wingspan almost equal to that of a B-52. These planes were never ordered into production, but when it was announced in 1983 that Northrop was building the stealth Advanced Technology Bomber (ATB), it wasn't hard to figure out what it might look like.

In 1987, it was announced that the Air Force would be buying 132 of the mysterious flying wings, which would be built at the highly secure factory complex at Palmdale in the California high desert. The first flight, scheduled for November 1987, was, however, postponed.

When the B-2 aircraft becomes operational in the early 1990s, it will mark the first time in over 30 years that the number of bombers in the Strategic Air Command inventory has enjoyed a significant increase. More significantly, the peculiar characteristics of the new bomber will give SAC a capability unparalleled among the world's air forces.

NORTHROP B-2 "STEALTH"

Wingspan:	172 ft.
Length:	69 ft.
Height:	17 ft.
Engines:	four General Electric F118 turbofans
Engine thrust (lbs.):	27,000–29,000
Gross weight (lbs.):	(classified)
Operating altitude (ft.):	(classified)
Crusing speed (mph):	500
Top speed (mph):	700
Maximum range (miles):	Intercontinental

The B-2 "Stealth" bomber unveiled in Palmdale, California. The jet uses an updated flying wing design and advanced technology to make it undetectable by radar. (Source: **UPI/ BETTMANN NEWSPHOTOS**)

RECON

Nose-on view of the SR-71.

RECONNAISSANCE AND ELECTRONIC WARFARE AIRCRAFT

There is something cool and mysterious about the environment of high-technology electronic warfare. Battles can be won and lost without a shot being fired. Secrets that took years to weave—and nearly as long to disguise—can be compromised in split seconds. On the other hand, guns and bombs can be understood. The roles of fighters, bombers, and transports are all self-evident. But what mysteries lurk beneath the epithet "spy" plane? Even the name conjures up an unknown world where nothing can be revealed.

Until after World War II, reconnaissance aircraft were mostly combat aircraft with their guns replaced by cameras. Recon birds based on fighters could go low and fast, while those adapted from bombers could provide imagery of strongholds well behind the front. The F-13 reconnaissance plane (a camera-equipped B-29) had to map the Japanese heartland prior to the big B-29 raids, because no accurate cartographic data about Japan existed in Allied files.

The idea of aircraft being used in electronic warfare is newer. As the technical complexity of radar defenses expands, so too must the means of defending against it. In Southeast Asia, the U.S. Air Force discovered that defense was as important as offense to the success of a bombing mission over heavily defended North Vietnam. Just as Air Force bombers developed weapons and tactics to defend against fighters, the Yanks over Hanoi found they had to deal with a North Vietnamese opponent that had the most sophisticated electronic defenses ever encountered in modern warfare. To meet this threat, and to be equally prepared to tackle well-defended potential targets in Eastern Europe, the Air Force converted about 20 B-66 tactical bombers to electronic-warfare aircraft. Armed with radar, electronic countermeasures hardware, and a ton of aluminum foil "chaff" (to fool enemy radar), the EB-66s accompanied American fighter-bombers on their raids.

The aerial-reconnaissance chore in Vietnam was handled by converted warplanes. In the early part of the Vietnam War, the RF-101 flew recon missions. This aircraft had distinguished itself in 1962 during the Cuban missile crisis. The RF-4C, the reconnaissance version of the great Phantom II fighter, replaced the RF-101 after 1967, and even today is state of the art for use in low-level, day-to-day tactical reconnaissance.

While converted aircraft can often do an admirable job, it is obvious that an aircraft specially designed for a specific task can meet that challenge to a greater degree. That is the case of today's reconnaissance aircraft, the Lockheed U-2/TR-1, the Lockheed SR-71 Blackbird, the Grumman E-2 Hawkeye, the Boeing E-3 Sentry (AWACS), and the Grumman EF-111 Raven, which are discussed in this section. They have discernible roots that are common with other airplanes, but in both appearance and application, these birds have evolved into some of the most incredible machines that ply the stratosphere.

The E-2 Hawkeye is carrier capable; its wings fold into a birdlike convolution for hangar deck storage.

The Lockheed TR-1 is a
larger and more powerful
variant of the U-2 design.

SR-71
BLACKBIRD

They say it's "faster than a speeding bullet," and that is *literally* true. After more than two decades of service, the Lockheed Blackbird is still the fastest airplane in the world. The X-15 was probably faster, but it hasn't flown in 20 years and it couldn't even take off by itself. Though the Blackbird has held the world's absolute speed record of 2,193.167 mph for over a decade, its actual top speed is much faster.

How fast?

It's top secret, but the SR-71 aircrews all wear patches that say "Mach 3-plus," and the emphasis is always on the plus. When you mention 4,000 mph around these same crews, there are usually a lot of knowing chuckles.

At a briefing given by the Ninth Strategic Reconnaissance Wing (which manages all the Blackbirds for the Air Force), a spokesperson was asked what they would do if someone—heaven forbid—ever took the speed record away from the SR-71. "We'd just take up one of our birds," he laughed, "and step down a little harder on the accelerator."

The Blackbird evolved from a Mach 3 interceptor, which had itself evolved from a CIA spy plane developed in the early 1960s. The mysterious Model A-12 reconnaissance airplane first flew in 1962, also a product of Lockheed's secret "Skunk Works" lab. In the meantime, Skunk Works boss Kelly Johnson had suggested that the Air Force might want to take a look at a Mach 3 interceptor version for its Air Defense Command (ADC). The Air Force brass came, looked, and bought. The YF-12 interceptor was the fastest such airplane ever flown, before or since. It could catch any enemy aircraft almost without regard to how much of a head start the other guy had. The YF-12 could cruise comfortably at three times the speed of sound, and it could outrun bullets!

The Strategic Air Command (SAC) looked at the ADC's wonderful new bird and decided that it was exactly what they needed as a new "Reconnaissance/Strike" airplane, and *they* ordered some under the designation RS-71. By the time SAC's airplane flew in 1964, reconnaissance was its sole function, and so its designation

was transposed to SR-71 for "Strategic Reconnaissance." The rest is history. The YF-12 subsequently went into mothballs, because the Secretary of Defense decided that the Soviets didn't have any bombers fast enough to pose any real challenge to it, and so the A-12's role was assumed by the SR-71.

It is a stunning airplane. From its design and engineering to the fuel that it burns in its engines, the Blackbird is like no other. The materials used in the construction of these airplanes were experimental at the time, and the overall design and shape of the fuselage (which provides most of the lift) were engineering breakthroughs.

The turboramjet engines, designed especially for these planes by Pratt & Whitney, are also unique. For sustained speeds of about Mach 3, they had to be. The SR-71 is the only airplane in the world known to burn JP-7 fuel, a concoction so *non*volatile that you can't light it with a match. It takes a chemical reaction to get the engines started.

One pilot described it this way: "When you strap this mother on, . . ." he said as the roar of the engines drowned him out. His point, however, was not lost. A Blackbird launch is like a space launch except that the SR-71 looks wilder and faster than any spacecraft ever flown.

From different angles, the Blackbird looks like three *different* spacecraft. From the side the SR-71 is an arrow; from the top the SR-71 is a hybrid pterodactyl; and from the front the SR-71 is three flying saucers in a row. The Blackbird sits on the runway like a prehistoric predator.

The crew arrives at the Blackbird in the same sort of flight suits worn by space shuttle astronauts. There are

(continued on p. 231)

Right: Wide-angle view of the SR-71's dramatically tapered nose.

(continued from p. 228)

two crew members: one who flies the bird and another who operates the cameras, sensors, and reconnaissance hardware. This equipment is secreted behind removable panels that are spread across the belly of the Blackbird. The exact nature of what is inside is secret, and the data collected does not go beyond the closed doors of the national-security establishment.

The heavy lids that secure the two cockpits are cranked down, the JP-7 is ignited, and the SR-71 shrieks down the runway. The Blackbird rolls out horizontally but takes off almost vertically and is out of sight in less time than it takes to tell about it.

Where will the SR-71 go? They'll never tell. The Blackbird could go all the way to Nicaragua and be back for lunch. The patrols of the Blackbird are secret, but the skies over Cuba and Nicaragua are familiar to its crews, and there are stories of it outrunning supersonic air-to-air missiles over North Korea and of cat-and-mouse games with MiGs off Vladivostok.

For all that the Blackbird is, though, it is most certainly black. Or is it? Even up close in broad daylight it is the purest form of light-absorbing, radar-absorbing flat black imaginable, yet in its Mach 3 world 20 miles above, the Blackbird is transformed into a deep indigo blue! As one pilot put it: "This is magic stuff."

The Blackbird is, as they say, "high '90s technology" that we were just lucky to have in the '60s. We are lucky to have the SR-71 now, and we will be lucky to have it in the high '90s, as well. By then, it will be fading, but not forgotten, and in the process of being replaced. We don't know what its successor will be, but we do know that it will have to be an amazing bird of "high 21st century technology."

LOCKHEED SR-71 BLACKBIRD

Wingspan:	55 ft. 7 in.
Length:	107 ft. 5 in.
Height:	18 ft. 6 in.
Engines:	two Pratt & Whitney J58 turboramjets
Engine thrust (lbs.):	32,500
Gross weight (lbs.):	172,000
Operating altitude (ft.):	100,000
Cruising speed (mph):	Mach 2.5 +
Top speed (mph):	Mach 3.5 +
Maximum range (miles):	3,250

Despite having put in more than a quarter-century of active service, the Blackbird remains the fastest and highest-flying military jet in the world.

A Blackbird makes its presence known preparatory to a flight that may take it higher than 100,000 feet and faster than Mach 4.

234

The Blackbird fleet is aging and will soon be permanently grounded. But for now, the awesome jets still fly, each with a crew of two.

E-2
HAWKEYE

The higher you climb a tree, the farther you can see. Radar, too, is "line of sight," meaning that the taller a radar mast, the longer the range of the radar. The radar mast on an aircraft carrier can stand as high as a 15-story building. The Grumman Hawkeye, however, has a radar mast that stands as high as a 2,500-story building. Suddenly, the true importance of the Hawkeye to modern naval warfare becomes crystal clear.

The Hawkeye does what its name implies: it manages the entire field of action for a carrier battle group from a vantage point high in the sky.

The idea of managing a battlefield from a command post in the sky was toyed with to varying degrees in both world wars. The early state of the art in communications and radar technology, however, kept the notion from coming to fruition until the 1950s. Naval aircraft, such as the land-based Lockheed WV-2 (EC-121 after 1962) Warning Star and the carrier-based Grumman WF-2 (E-1 after 1962) Tracer, were among the early successes. Both Navy and Air Force EC-121s served in Vietnam, where they refined the techniques for large-scale airborne battlefield control that ultimately led to the E-3 AWACS.

Based on the S-2 Tracker, the E-1 Tracer proved that the concept of a carrier-based Airborne Early Warning (AEW)/flying command post was a workable idea. However, initially it was limited by the sophistication of its radar, and there was not enough room aboard the Tracer for the high-speed digital computer necessary to sort out the haze of blips on the radar screen. In 1957, the Navy picked Grumman to develop a larger and more capable aircraft. The result was a turboprop-powered airplane with only a passing resemblance to the Tracer. It was called Hawkeye and made its first flight in 1960.

Originally designated W2F, Hawkeye was redesignated as E-2 in 1962 before entering service in 1964. The current standard Hawkeye is the E-2C, which entered service aboard the Navy's carriers in 1974. Of this type, over 100 have been built, with more on the way. Not only has the U.S. Navy been buying Hawkeyes but several have gone to Egypt and Japan as well as Israel, which used them to great advantage in the 1982 air war with Syria and in general surveillance of its precarious borders.

The Hawkeye's most distinguishing feature is its huge, saucerlike radome perched delicately above its back. To compensate for the airflow from this unusual appendage, Grumman engineers gave the plane a tail with not one, but four vertical tail surfaces. The 24-foot radome revolves once every ten seconds, while providing its own lift.

Beneath the spinning dome, a three-member AEW crew works, while a two-member flight crew directs the Hawkeye on its appointed rounds. The crew—including an air traffic controller—can see more than 200 miles in any direction. Within the dome, the APA-171 radar sees all. It has a surveillance envelope of *three million cubic miles.* The system can handle more than 600 airborne targets and can track ships and ground vehicles at the same time. Hunched over their flickering screens, the AEW crew can control and direct 40 intercept operations simultaneously.

Typically, each carrier airwing will have an AEW squadron equipped with four Hawkeyes. There are additional AEW squadrons at land bases from Atsugi in Japan to Miramar in California. In Florida, Hawkeyes have been assigned to help in the effort to defeat smuggling into the United States by cocaine traffickers.

GRUMMAN E-2C HAWKEYE

Wingspan:	80 ft. 7 in.
Length:	57 ft. 6¾ in.
Height:	18 ft. 3¾ in.
Engines:	two Allison T56-A-425 turboprops
Engine (hp):	4,910
Maximum T-O weight (lbs.):	51,933
Operating altitude (ft.):	30,800
Cruising speed (mph):	308
Top speed (mph):	372
Maximum range (miles):	1,605

Right: The 24-foot radome atop the E-2C Hawkeye generates enough aerodynamic lift to compensate for its weight and drag.

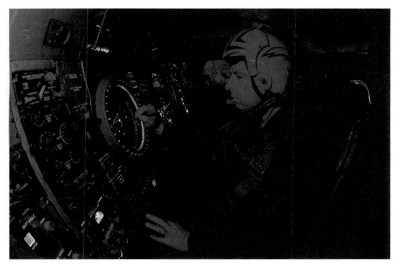

Left: During normal carrier operations, a Hawkeye's radars and three operators will scan a couple million cubic miles of sea and sky. *Above:* Illuminated by the glow from their sophisticated equipment, Hawkeye operators perform their vital work.

E-3
SENTRY

Floating lazily through the sky like an airliner being followed by a friendly flying saucer, the Boeing E-3 Sentry is actually the most sophisticated airborne command post ever devised. A handful of them could control operations throughout Europe.

During the Vietnam War, the U.S. Air Force flew its *College Eye* EC-121Qs and the remarkable *Igloo White* EC-121R Batcats over Laos and the Gulf of Tonkin, and had great success in controlling and directing air operations against North Vietnam. After the war, a revolution in electronics made possible far more sophistication in much less space, and the Air Force went for even *more* space and the capability that it provided.

The airframe chosen was the Boeing Model 707 type, which was similar to the 717 and 739 airframes of the already extant Air Force KC-135s, RC-135s, and EC-135s. This airframe was, in turn, designed to be configured with the leading edge of state-of-the-art electronics, and then topped off with a 30-foot rotating radome. The big skunk-striped "rotodome" is similar to, though larger than, the one on Grumman's E-2 Hawkeye and is backed up with a more than proportionally greater information processing capability. The result was the Air Force Airborne Warning And Control System (AWACS), built into an airplane designated E-3 and called Sentry because of its job, which, quite simply, is to stand guard.

The first of two dozen E-3A Sentrys were delivered in 1977, and they went to work on the first day of 1979. Though owned and flown by the Air Force Tactical Air Command (TAC), their first, and continuing, assignment is with the joint U.S./Canadian North American Air Defense Command (NORAD), guarding the periphery of this vast continent.

A round of updating began to turn the E-3As into E-3Bs and E-3Cs in 1984. The improvements included increasing the number of situation display consoles (SDC), improving the Have Quick radar jammers, and upgrading the Joint Tactical Information Distribution System (JTIDS) and Tactical Digital Information Link (TADIL). When TADIL tattles, the crew members at the SDC listen, and the more clearly they hear, the safer everyone is.

As the world discovered when an Iranian airliner was shot down by mistake in the Persian Gulf in July 1988, battlefield electronics are only as good as the peo-

ple who operate them, and decisions are only as good as the precision of the information upon which they are based. This makes IFF (Identification, Friend or Foe) recognition a vital part of the AWACS chore, a chore that is made all that much harder by the theaters in which the E-3 must operate. North America has some of the heaviest concentrations of air traffic anywhere, although the areas of concern to TAC and NORAD are on the periphery, where traffic is lighter.

In Europe, however, things are vastly more complex. Here, we find the air forces and airlines of two dozen nations divided almost arbitrarily down the center in the heart of the thickest morass of air traffic on earth. To complicate matters, commercial flights can cross the line at certain points, but military flights can't cross anywhere. How do you know whether the radar blip that crossed at the wrong point is an airliner off course or a bad guy? It's not easy, but the Sentry can do it. It *has* to.

Most of the world's E-3s operate in Europe. NATO owns 18 of them, both Britain and France have them on order, and the U.S. Air Force always has some of its Sentrys on hand. In time of war, these planes would have to form an interlocking, yet noninterfering, network of command posts that could manage the hundreds of NATO warplanes that would be airborne at any given moment. These, in turn, would have to be distinguished from enemy and neutral aircraft. The bad guys might be trying to look like good guys, and the neutral aircraft might be flying pretty erratic patterns, panicking and trying not to get hit. On the other hand, there might be some bad guys pretending to be neutral, hoping that the good guys think twice before pulling the trigger.

In any case, the situation at the display consoles aboard an E-3 during the opening day of World War III would resemble the floor of the New York Stock Exchange

(continued on p. 242)

Right: The civilian-707 ancestry of the E-3A Sentry is obvious in this airstrip view.

(continued from p. 240)

on Black Monday. It would make the air traffic control center at O'Hare Airport look like a desert island. The IBM CC-2 computers that are the heart of each Sentry's data processing capability would have to function flawlessly and use most of their ability to perform a quarter million operations per second.

In the end, it will all come down to the skill and tenacity of the men and women sitting at those consoles. Tools change and tools evolve, but in the high-tech bullpen of Sentry, the human quotient is the bottom line—not unlike the plain at Marathon or the Flanders Field.

BOEING E-3 SENTRY (AWACS)

Wingspan:	145 ft. 9 in.
Length:	152 ft. 11 in.
Height:	41 ft. 9 in.
Engines:	four Pratt & Whitney TF33-PW-100/100A turbofans
Engine thrust (lbs.):	21,000
Maximum T-O weight (lbs.):	325,000
Operating altitude (ft.):	29,000
Top speed (mph):	530
Maximum range (miles):	7,475

Radar receivers connected to antennas inside the E-3A's rotating radome can scan several million cubic miles of airspace.

EF-111
RAVEN

It doesn't look much like a Raven. Who ever heard of a *gray* raven that looks like an F-111 with a football bolted to its tail?

In fact, this aircraft has more in common with an EA-6 Prowler than with an F-111 Aardvark. As for the fuzzy, warm gray paint—well, it sucks up radar like a sponge. That's the EF-111 story in a nutshell.

During the Vietnam War, the radar environment in downtown Hanoi got to be so thick that the F-105 fighter-bombers that went north took EB-66s along for the sole purpose of jamming enemy radar. Based on this experience and the success of these operations, the Air Force decided in the early 1970s to refine the concept and develop a successor to the EB-66.

The F-111 airframe was picked for its low-level capability, its "swing-wing" flexibility, and the fact that the jamming aircraft would probably be escorting F-111 and FB-111 bombers. With basic engines and airframes in common, the jammer and its bombers could be maintained by the same team, and their similar flight characteristics could very well be the deciding factor in the success of a mission. Grumman, with its expertise in developing the E-1, E-2, and EA-6 for the Navy, was chosen to rewire and modify over 40 of the old 'Varks.

Flight testing began in 1977, and the Ravens were deployed overseas to the RAF base at Upper Heyford in England in 1984 as components of the 42nd Electronic Combat Squadron.

Two years later, in April 1986, when F-111s were deployed against bases in Libya, three EF-111s went along. Although the intended mission of the F-111/EF-111 team is deep interdiction within Eastern Europe in wartime, they answered the requirements of the Libyan job and could do so again.

Whether it is east of Budapest or north of Beirut, wherever an Aardvark is sent to kick a bad guy, he'll have a Raven on his shoulder.

GRUMMAN EF-111A RAVEN	
Wingspan (unswept):	63 ft.
Wingspan (swept):	31 ft. 11½ in.
Length:	76 ft.
Height:	20 ft.
Engines:	two Pratt & Whitney TF30-P-30 turbofans
Engine thrust (lbs.):	18,500
Maximum T-O weight (lbs.):	88,948
Operating altitude (ft.):	45,000
Cruising speed (mph):	514
Top speed (mph):	1,412
Maximum range (miles):	2,303

Right: **The electronics wizard aboard the EF-111 "Spark 'Vark" uses radar to jam the fire-control systems of enemy anti-aircraft missile batteries.**

TRANSPORTS

Early C-5s were painted in this handsome scheme.

The transportation of materiel and personnel—the science and art of logistics—is essential to any military operation. Napoleon said that an army marches on its stomach, and that dictum is no less true now than it was in 1813. Furthermore, weapons, from handguns to B-52s, are no better than the ability of their users to supply them with ammunition.

Just as wars are fought by military forces on land, sea, and air, so too are those forces supplied by land, sea, and air. On land, the process would involve rail and road transportation. The responsibility to supply forces overseas goes to the transport ships of the U.S. Navy's Military Sealift Command and the civilian transports that are pressed into service in wartime. In the air, the job falls largely to the U.S. Air Force Military Airlift Command (MAC) and the civilian airliners that are used on a contract basis to supplement its capacity. As such, MAC is the focus of our attention.

Of the more than 900 aircraft in the MAC fleet, more than three-quarters are of the three specialized types discussed in this section: the Lockheed C-130 Hercules, the Lockheed C-141 Starlifter, and the Lockheed C-5 Galaxy. The remainder are of a wide array of types that are, for the most part, military derivations of civilian airliner or general aviation types. These include the McDonnell Douglas C-9 ambulance planes, which are based on the DC-9 jetliner; the Beechcraft C-12s, which are based on the Super King Air 200; the Grumman C-20s, which are off-the-shelf Gulfstream IIs; the C-21s, which are Learjet 35s; the Boeing C-22s, which are used 727 jetliners; and the C-23s, which are all-freight versions of the Shorts 300 small regional airliner.

An important part of MAC's job—outside the military airlift role—is to provide executive transportation for government officials, notably the President of the United States. This task is carried out by MAC's 89th Military Airlift Wing (MAW) at Andrews AFB near Washington, D.C. Any airplane that carries the President would be assigned the call sign *Air Force One*. For the last quarter century, that airplane was almost always one of the 89th's five VC-137s.

From 1948 until 1965, when MAC was created, the Air Force transport command was called the Military Air Transport Service (MATS). During much of this time, the Navy operated the Naval Air Transport Service (NATS), a competing transporter that duplicated some of MATS effort. Part of the idea behind MAC was to consolidate most of the United States military airlift into one command.

Today, MAC hauls cargo for the Navy and Marines, as well as for the Air Force and Army. All the services, including the Coast Guard, still use the C-130 for specialized purposes, however. The Navy also has its own C-9 ambulance planes and a few C-12s for utility purposes. Aside from these, the only transports peculiar to the Navy are the Grumman C-1 Trader and the newer C-2 Greyhound (now replacing the C-1).

The C-1, based on the old S-2 Tracker, has a cargo capacity of less than two tons. The C-2, a variant of the E-2 Hawkeye, can carry five tons of payload. These unique transports are used for Carrier On-board Delivery (COD), in other words, for carrying supplies and personnel between aircraft carriers and between shore bases and carriers.

While most of the Air Force and Navy planes discussed above (excluding the C-9s and those of the 89th MAW) can generally be classified as "small" aircraft in terms of load-carrying capability, the three Lockheeds that make up the bulk of MAC were carefully planned to meet the need for "medium," "large," and "extra large" transports. While a small transport can carry a four-ton load, the medium C-130 Hercules can carry 25 tons, the large C-141 Starlifter 45 tons, and the extra-large C-5 Galaxy can haul up to 150 tons of payload.

The story of contemporary American military transports is also the story of the Military Airlift Command, its capability and its operations around the globe.

(continued on p. 253)

Above: **The Air National Guard HC-130 provides search-and-rescue services from its Moffett Field, California, base.** *Right:* **Maintenance workers swarm over a Marine Corps KC-130.**

C-130
HERCULES

The C-130 is one of the most remarkable airplanes in the U.S. Air Force. Still in production at Lockheed's plant in Marietta, Georgia, after 35 years, more than 1,800 C-130s have been delivered. And more are on the way. This durable airlifter has played a role in virtually every American military operation during that time and has been in continuous service in every part of the world where American military forces have been.

The Hercules made its first flight in 1954, introducing a new age of turboprop-powered Air Force transports. Soon, not only the Air Force but the Navy, the Marines, and the Coast Guard were lining up to acquire C-130s. Eventually, more than 50 foreign air forces from Abu Dhabi to Zaire also bought the Hercules.

There are currently about 700 C-130s in the Air Force, divided more or less equally between active Military Airlift Command units and reserve and Air Guard units assigned to MAC. Most of these are C-130B and C-130E transports, along with some newer C-130Hs and HC-130Hs that are assigned to MAC's Rescue & Recovery Service. The Navy, Marines, and Coast Guard together operate about 100 Hercules in various roles, ranging from the Coast Guard's HC-130H rescue aircraft to the ski-equipped Navy LC-130s used in Antarctica and the KC-130s that the Marine Corps uses for aerial refueling.

Nor is this the extent of the "Herk's" many-faceted repertoire. While the majority of America's C-130 fleet is moving cargo or performing one of many routine tasks, others are unobtrusively, and often secretly, completing nearly unimaginable missions:

Somewhere over the Pacific, a JHC-130 snares a film capsule in midair from a spy satellite streaking through the earth's atmosphere.

In a world trouble-spot, a DC-130 is an airborne aircraft carrier, clutching four one-ton remote-control airplanes beneath its wings. On cue, these unmanned drones silently fly off into the twilight to snap photos by infrared light of guerrillas in a jungle. Subjected to small arms fire, the drones may die, but the DC-130 will be long gone.

Deep in hostile territory, an MC-130 Combat Talon—belonging to an Air Force Special Operations Squadron—pushes through a nighttime rainstorm to retrieve a friendly operative from a hiding place. The MC-130 comes in very low, extends huge scissorslike whiskers from its nose, and tightens a cable. The MC-130 snatches a second cable that is attached to the secret agent and

(continued on p. 253)

Right: The Air Force Reserve uses this aging WC-130 Hercules out of Keesler AFB, Mississippi, for punishing hurricane-watch flights into the eye of the huge storms.

(continued from p. 250)

held aloft by a helium balloon. With a sudden snap, he's off the ground and airborne beneath the MC-130.

In a hurricane's eye, all is quiet. Suddenly, a form emerges from the 150-mph winds embodying the fury of the hurricane. Its nothing supernatural, it's just a WC-130 making a routine penetration of the storm to obtain weather-forecasting data.

And finally, it's time for Spectre, a Herk so far removed from the original C-130 freighter that it has become an *attack* plane with the heaviest guns currently equipping an American aircraft. The Spectre gunship was born in 1967 in Vietnam, the grandson of Spooky. In 1965, the Air Force needed an aircraft that could pour a concentrated wall of gunfire at a ground target for prolonged periods of time. With forward-firing guns, the best that even the slowest aircraft could do was a few seconds—that is, until 1965, when Spooky was born.

Known originally as "Puff the Magic Dragon" (or "Dragon Ship") because of the smoke it breathed, Spooky was a 30-year-old C-47 transport with *side-firing* cannons and machine guns. The Dragon Ships were the original gunships. They were able to concentrate their firepower by orbiting the target in a circular pattern so that the lines of fire were focused—like spokes of a wheel—on a single target point for 20 minutes without pause. It was a simple, yet revolutionary, solution to the problem. Within two years the AC-47s were augmented and eventually replaced by C-119 Flying Boxcars, revised as AC-119 Shadow and Stinger gunships.

In 1967, the AC-130 Spectre gunships were deployed; they carried 20-millimeter, 40-millimeter, and even 75-millimeter cannons. After the war, the AC-130s remained and evolved. Today, the AC-130H is the penultimate Spectre, with a 105-millimeter howitzer in place. By the end of the decade, the AC-130U will be on line with a deadly combination of 25-millimeter, 40-millimeter, and 105-millimeter cannons directed by sophisticated low-light TV and infrared target locators.

From transport to gunship, from electronic warfare to airborne battlefield control, who would have pictured a 35-year-old turboprop to be the prime candidate for a one-airplane air force!

LOCKHEED C-130H HERCULES

Wingspan:	132 ft. 7 in.
Length:	97 ft. 9 in.
Height:	38 ft. 3 in.
Engines:	four Allison T56-A-15 turboprops
Engine (hp):	4,508
Maximum T-O weight (lbs.):	155,000
Operating altitude (ft.):	33,000
Cruising speed (mph):	345
Top speed (mph):	375
Maximum range (miles):	4,894

The Hercules can span oceans and then land on an unimproved dirt runway in only a few hundred feet.

The KC-130 Hercs are the refueling planes for the Marine Corps. They double as troop and cargo carriers.

Left: The support aircraft for the Navy's *Blue Angels* is a Herc nicknamed "Fat Albert." It occasionally puts on its own flashy performance for air show crowds, making high-angle jet-assisted takeoff departures with eight disposable rocket motors attached to its fuselage. *Above:* Through this fuselage blister, the Herc's navigator often practices with an old-fashioned nautical sextant.

C-141
STARLIFTER

With the three-tone, gray-green "European One" paint scheme that the Lockheed C-141 has worn since the mid-1980s, it has earned the nickname "lizard." It's just a disguise—the C-141 is really the Military Airlift Command's airliner. Its old livery of crisp gray and black with a full-color MAC logo on its tail really fit it better because it's the jetliner that flies MAC's routine schedule across the globe.

The Starlifter's typical day might begin with a take-off from Travis AFB near San Francisco, home of the 60th Military Airlift Wing. Passengers and cargo are bound for points west—with service people from all the branches eating a box lunch over the Pacific. The C-141 stops at Hickam AFB in Hawaii—some passengers get off, a few more get on—then the plane flies across the international date line and on to Andersen AFB in Guam.

The next stop is Clark AB in the Philippines. The crew changes, and more passengers bound for the north get on, to Kadena AB on Okinawa. The Starlifter goes on to Yokota AB near Tokyo, and the C-141 then completes the great circle. Having crossed the date line bound for Travis, the C-141 is home before it left Yokota.

Already other C-141s are in the loop—Hickam to Andersen to Clark. It's the same in the Atlantic loop—flying out of Dover AFB in Delaware or McGuire AFB in New Jersey to RAF Alconbury or Rhein-Main AB in Germany.

The Starlifter may be one of the least glamorous birds in the Air Force, but MAC could not do its job without the C-141. It is the everyday airliner of the military airline.

It's a job that the Starlifter was born to do back in 1963 when it made its initial voyage. The Starlifter was designed to be an airlifter in the same size and weight class as the largest commercial jetliners of the day. The C-141—with its shoulder-mounted wings for operation from less than perfect runways, the cargo ramp in its aft fuselage, and its lack of windows—was unlike any commercial jetliner. The C-141 was also designed to accommodate the weight and bulk of Minuteman ICBMs. No jetliner ever had to meet *that* spec.

The Starlifter entered squadron service in 1965, just as the Vietnam War was heating up and just when it was necessary to have an airlifter that could fly nonstop from California to Saigon. The C-141's airline days began with routine flights to routine airports, while its cousin,

the C-130, was saving the Marines with daredevil landings on rugged mountaintops.

Lockheed built a total of 285 Starlifters. Unlike the C-130, which was sold to every American service and to two dozen countries around the world, Lockheed would have but one customer for the C-141.

As the 1970s wore on, however, it became clear that the Starlifter was not living up to its billing. Designed to tote the 41-ton Minuteman, most of the C-141's routine loads were averaging much less because of a lack of volume. In 1976, every C-141 in the fleet was stretched by 23 feet (a pair of fuselage sections ahead and behind the wing roots were added). By 1982, all 267 remaining Starlifters had been lengthened, retrofitted with hardware to make them aerial refuelable, and redesignated C-141B. The volume was increased so the payload weight started living up to the Starlifter's promise.

In foul weather or fair, the Starlifter is there—meeting the schedules, hauling the goods, dropping paratroopers, and fulfilling MAC's commitments around the world.

LOCKHEED C-141B STARLIFTER

Wingspan:	159 ft. 11 in.
Length:	168 ft. 3½ in.
Height:	39 ft. 3½ in.
Engines:	four Pratt & Whitney TF33-P-7 turbofans
Engine thrust (lbs.):	21,000
Gross weight (lbs.):	343,000
Operating altitude (ft.):	25,000
Cruising speed (mph):	566
Top speed (mph):	570
Maximum range (miles):	4,080

Right: **In addition to routine transport chores, C-141 Starlifter aircrews practice more dangerous tactical missions, including aerial refueling and evasive, low-level flying.**

The C-141 is the Air Force's highly successful medium-lift transport, and the mainstay of the "airline" known as the Military Airlift Command.

C-5
GALAXY

For 17 years, the Galaxy was the biggest airplane in the world (until the Soviet Union's Antonov An-124 made its debut in 1985, with a tail core that made it five feet longer). Nevertheless, no airplane on earth has ever come closer to a million-pound gross weight than the Galaxy.

When you walk into the Lockheed C-5's gargantuan cargo bay, it's more like walking into a hangar than into an airplane. There is a ramp in the aft under the huge seven-story tail and there's another one in the nose so that you can drive in one end and out the other. Which end is which? It doesn't matter; there's room for two lanes of traffic, one going in each direction!

In this bay there is room for 16 army trucks or more than two dozen compact cars. (It's high enough that you could load 50 compact cars two-deep in trailers.) There's room for 36 standard shipping pallets, versus 22 in a McDonnell Douglas DC-10 freighter or 29 in a Boeing 747 freighter. Two 60-ton Abrams tanks could fit here comfortably—and frequently they do. Six Apache attack helicopters can also be carried, as can ten Pershing missiles or a couple of ICBMs. Military Airlift Command has even hauled some of the Navy's smaller submarines in a C-5.

There's also room for people in the C-5. The aft passenger compartment alone can carry the same number as a Boeing 727. Overall, there's room for 80 basketball teams. In fact, if you moved the cargo out and closed the doors, you'd have almost enough room for a regulation basketball court. And with the range of the Galaxy, there would be enough time for most of those 80 teams to play at least one quarter.

The climb from the floor of the cargo bay to the flight deck is like climbing the stairs in a three-story building. The flight deck is, in turn, like a small apartment. There is a nice gallery and dining area reminiscent of a Pullman car. There are enough bunks for a complete extra flight crew and a rest area for 15 crew members. The pilot and copilot fly the Galaxy in a space too much like a comfortable-size living room to be described as a "cockpit." Even with eight people standing around, it doesn't feel crowded.

The remarkable Galaxy was born amid controversy over its cost and performance, and made its first flight in 1968. At that time, nobody had ever built an airplane so big (the first Boeing 747 was still under construction). Low price estimates proved costly for Lockheed. Delays and cost overruns resulted in Congress funding only 81 of the originally planned 115 C-5As. Nevertheless, they reached MAC squadrons in time for limited service during the Vietnam War.

By the end of the 1970s, the C-5A had performed such feats as having parachute-dropped 80 tons of cargo in a *single* mission and *air-launching* a Minuteman ICBM. The entire fleet logged 400,000 hours and hauled four billion tons of cargo. In 1980, the C-5A fleet was retrofitted with new wing components to give each airframe another 30,000 hours of flight time.

Even with the increased longevity being built into the C-5A, there was still a serious need for more heavy airlift capacity within the MAC fleet. In 1982, Congress agreed to let the Air Force buy 50 more Galaxys. Designated C-5B, the new planes are similar in appearance to the C-5As but have stronger wings, bigger engines, and improved avionics. The first C-5B, resplendent in its gray-green European One camouflage scheme, joined MAC in 1986, to be followed by the 50th in 1989.

The fact that you can carry 50 compact cars or play basketball inside a Galaxy is a useful means of suggesting the scale of an individual aircraft. In an overall sense, though, it is more useful to compare what contribution the total fleet of such huge planes has made to MAC's

(continued on p. 264)

Right: **Nose shot of a C-5A Galaxy, the largest aircraft in the free world.**

(continued from p. 262)

overall heavy-lift capability. For example, the entire C-130 transport fleet can lift 12,300 tons, and the entire C-141B fleet can lift 11,700 tons. The combined Galaxy fleet will be able to lift 19,000 tons with vastly fewer individual flights.

It is this sheer load-carrying power that will make the Galaxy an integral part of the MAC for the rest of the century, just as the Galaxy and all of its Lockheed brethren continue to make MAC the most potent military airlift force in the world.

LOCKHEED C-5B GALAXY

Wingspan:	222 ft. 8½ in.
Length:	247 ft. 10 in.
Height:	65 ft. 1½ in.
Engines:	four General Electric TF39-GE-1C turbofans
Engine thrust (lbs.):	43,000
Maximum T-O weight (lbs.):	837,000
Operating altitude (ft.):	35,750
Cruising speed (mph):	518
Top speed (mph):	564
Maximum range (miles):	6,469

The C-5A's hinged nose and tail ramp permit simultaneous loading and unloading.

265

Above, top: The Galaxy is powered by a quartet of General Electric turbofans, each of which puts out more than 40,000 pounds of thrust. *Above, bottom:* The C-5A's capacious flight deck. *Right:* Although Russia's AN-124 Condor is a few inches longer in wingspan and body size, the C-5A cuts an imposing figure.

TANKERS

A KC-10 Extender at sunset.

The concept of refueling one airplane from another would no doubt have intrigued the Wright Brothers, but it wasn't until after the first World War that somebody was crazy enough to try it. By 1929, the once-crude technique had evolved to a point where a group of U.S. Army Air Corps flyers undertook a nonstop transcontinental flight from Oakland to New York using a Boeing Model 95 mail plane called *Hornet Shuttle.* Several Boeing Model 40Bs were equipped with extra large-capacity fuel tanks and long hoses and positioned at Elko, Nevada; Cheyenne, Wyoming; Omaha, Nebraska; and Cleveland, Ohio. As the *Hornet Shuttle* came close, a tanker plane went up to greet it, a hose was dropped, grabbed by hand, and the extra tank drained into the thirsty Boeing 95.

This stunt was the high-water mark for aerial refueling for nearly two decades. After World War II, the USAAF (U.S. Air Force after 1947) decided to try some experiments in which fuel was transferred between two Boeing B-29s by the same method that had been used in 1929. What had worked as a stunt in the open-cockpit biplane days proved to be impractical with huge, pressurized strategic bombers. But, finally, in 1948, Boeing developed the "flying boom," a rigid pipe that could be extended from one airplane to another.

KB-29 tankers were first used to support aircraft in combat—both bombers and fighters—during the Korean War. In 1951, Boeing began delivery of KC-97 tankers, which were variations of the Stratocruiser airliner. They had roughly the same overall dimensions as the KB-29 but a greater fuselage *volume* and, hence, greater fuel capacity. Though the KC-97 remained in service with reserve units until the 1970s, it was replaced, beginning in the mid-1950s, by the queen of all aerial refueling aircraft, the KC-135.

Today, the U.S. Air Force has the largest aerial refueling fleet in the world. The Air Force is also one of only two major services in the world that use the flying boom method of refueling. Only the French *Armee de Air* uses the flying boom, while the Canadian Armed Forces, the British Royal Air Force, and the U.S. Navy all use the "hose and drogue" method. Essentially, this method is a variation on the old 1929 Air Corps experiment that was refined by the RAF in the late 1940s.

In the hose and drogue method, the refueler unreels a hose with a little cup (drogue) dragging at the end. The airplane to be refueled has a probe that snaps out from the side of the nose, pokes into the little cup, and starts the fuel flowing. The advantage of this method is that several tanks may be carried by the refueler, thus allowing it to refuel several airplanes—a brace of fighters, for instance—simultaneously.

In the last four decades, aerial refueling has shown itself to be one of the most important innovations in the deployment of combat aircraft. Huge, lumbering gas tanks in the sky help extend the range of smaller aircraft and give larger aircraft virtually unlimited range. In a combat situation, an aircraft may push its engines to the limit of its performance. Although this may be a vital necessity for completing the mission, full power gulps a tremendous volume of fuel in an amazingly short time. When it comes down to a hard choice between running out of gas or completing the mission, it may be useful for a fighter jockey to know that there will be a big, friendly tanker waiting out there to top off the tanks!

The seemingly impossible is made routine. A Navy CH-53's huge seven-blade rotor comes close to a Hercules' tail during refueling.

KC-135
STRATOTANKER

The twin sister of the world's first successful jetliner, the KC-135 has refueled more airplanes in midair than most airports have refueled on the ground.

When jet-propelled military aircraft arrived on the scene during the final days of World War II, it was confidently predicted that commercial jets were just around the corner. There were, however, more corners than expected. The first jetliner, Britain's de Havilland Comet, didn't go into service until 1952, and then a series of disastrous crashes forced British Overseas Airways to withdraw it from service. In the United States, all the major airliner builders except Boeing took heed and were wary about rushing into development of a jetliner.

Boeing's only commercial program, the Stratocruiser, was marginally successful and the company felt it had nothing to lose. Almost all their business consisted of building big jet bombers for the Air Force, so they had a certain expertise already in place that could prove quite useful in a jetliner program. There was also hope that the Air Force would now be ready for a jet transport.

The whole project was conducted in strictest secrecy. The prototype Boeing jetliner was even given a Stratocruiser model number, yet the airplane that emerged in 1954 was anything but a Stratocruiser. Designated as Model 367-80, a.k.a. "Dash Eighty," the new airplane was actually the prototype for *two* aircraft types. One branch of the "Dash Eighty's" lineage would become the Model 707 jetliner, while the other would become the Model 717, which entered the Air Force as the C-135, and soon also as the KC-135. The 707 rewrote commercial aviation history, and the 717 became the first military jet transport. The KC-135 is often incorrectly identified as a "military 707" but it is really a 717.

The timing for both airplanes was just about perfect. The 707 was virtually the world's *only* jetliner for several critical years, and the 717 arrived at precisely the same moment that the bulk of the Strategic Air Command's B-52 fleet was coming on-line. The old Boeing KC-97 tankers (based on the Stratocruiser) couldn't keep pace with the B-52s, but the 717 *could.* The Air Force ordered some 717s as C-135 transports, but of 820 717s ordered, 732 became KC-135 tankers. The Air Force also ordered a few 707s, that received the military designation C-137.

Given the name Stratotanker, the KC-135 entered service with SAC in 1957, and has been at work ever since. During the Vietnam War, KC-135s were the deciding factor in countless missions over North Vietnam. Though equipped with a flying boom, the Stratotanker can also deploy a hose and drogue for refueling U.S. Navy aircraft, a characteristic that proved very useful in Southeast Asia.

Today, the KC-135 fleet, which is entirely owned by SAC, still supports not only the Air Force but the Navy and the Marine Corps as well. This fleet consists primarily of the original KC-135As, but since 1982 many of them have been receiving major systems modifications and are being retrofitted with more efficient and quieter General Electric/SNECMA turbofan engines. As each KC-135A is so modified, it will be redesignated KC-135R. Other KC-135As that are assigned to SAC reserve units are being reengined with surplus Pratt & Whitney turbofans under the designation KC-135E. There are also several dozen (the exact number is a secret) Stratotankers designated as KC-135Q that carry the special JP-7 fuel used only by the SR-71 reconnaissance aircraft.

Close relatives to the 707/717 family are the EC-135 and RC-135 special duty aircraft. Most are actually converted KC-135s, but 14 RC-135s were specially built under the Boeing 739 model number. EC-135s have been used for a quarter century as airborne command posts for the various Air Force commands. The EC-135s belonging to the Strategic Air Command, code-named *Looking Glass,* have been in the air (albeit, in shifts) continuously for that many years. The idea is that if SAC's control center on the ground in Omaha were to be destroyed, the high-level team aboard Looking Glass would pick up the task of managing the command's global assets. To aid in

(continued on p. 275)

Right: **The KC-135 Stratotanker refueler at work, viewed from the back seat of an F-16 Falcon.**

(continued from p. 272)

these long-duration missions, EC-135s retain the refueling capability that they had as KC-135s. This way, Looking Glass ships can refuel each other as well as other aircraft.

The RC-135s are distinguished by strangely shaped noses and bulges on their sides that contain powerful electronic surveillance gear, among which is the world's largest airborne steerable antenna. They are frequently found along the perimeters of the Soviet Union, monitoring missile test telemetry and similar "secret" operations.

The basic 707/717 airframe is as durable today as it was revolutionary 40 years ago. Its versatility led to the EC-135 and RC-135 and, ultimately, to the E-3 Sentry AWACS. But its real significance to the Air Force lies with the way the KC-135 tankers have enhanced the ability of all the other aircraft to do their jobs more effectively.

BOEING KC-135R STRATOTANKER

Wingspan:	130 ft. 10 in.
Length:	136 ft. 3 in.
Height:	38 ft. 4 in.
Engines:	four General Electric F108-CF-100 turbofans
Engine thrust (lbs.):	22,000
Maximum T-O weight (lbs.):	322,500
Operating altitude (ft.):	41,000
Cruising speed (mph):	600
Maximum range (miles):	5,000

A Stratotanker refuels a gas-hungry B-52 BUFF, one of the very few Air Force jets that dwarfs the KC-135.

Above: The Stratotanker's boom operator lies face-down on a couch in the rear of the tanker and uses hand controls to "fly" the fuel boom toward its target. *Right:* The boom of a KC-135 is maneuvered toward the fuel port of a thirsty aircraft.

Above, top: The photographer's F-16B waits in "pre-contact" position as the wingman approaches the Stratotanker's pipe. *Above, bottom:* The nearly 800 Stratotankers operated by the Air Force form the backbone of SAC's refueling fleet. *Right:* The KC-135 is a superb performer that was developed from the Boeing 707 jetliner. "R"-model versions that sport powerful French-built turbofans will probably serve for several more decades.

KC-10
EXTENDER

In a KC-135 Stratotanker, the refueling boom is operated by a crew member lying face down on a cramped leather couch peering out a small window. Compare this with a scene where the operator sits in what amounts to a huge armchair poised before a picture window. There is no comparison. The boom operator hasn't died and gone to heaven, he's just been transferred to a KC-10.

The KC-135s may be the backbone of SAC's worldwide refueling fleet, but the KC-10s are the glittering jewels. There will never be enough of them—only 53 were built—to compete with the Stratotanker for omnipresence, but they, too, have a unique role to play.

Take, for example, a situation where a fighter squadron suddenly has to go overseas. They can get in the air and find a way to get there, but what about supplies, equipment, and support personnel? Does the squadron hope that it will be on the next plane, or that they'll be able to scrape something together on the other end? Not with the KC-10. The aptly named Extender is the ideal helpmate in a situation such as this. Not only can a couple of KC-10s go with the fighters nonstop to keep their tanks full en route but the squadron can throw all their gear into the big plane's cargo hold and take everything along!

The KC-10's basic airframe is identical to that of the commercial DC-10 airliner. The major differences are, of course, the boom and the boom operator's station and the near-complete absence of windows. The area that is configured with passenger seats in a DC-10 is left wide open in the KC-10, with provisions for bolting in portable seats or tying down cargo pallets. Huge fuel bladders have been installed along the entire lower deck of the KC-10, with a capacity of 200,000 pounds of jet fuel.

First flown in 1980, a decade after the first DC-10s went into service, the KC-10 was born into a world in which nearly 40 airlines were using DC-10s. This means that KC-10 crews are likely to find parts and support facilities in places they might never have dreamed of having to look for them. The commonality between the DC-10 and KC-10 also means that Air Force Reserve KC-10 pilots who fly DC-10s are staying in practice for both jobs all the time!

McDONNELL DOUGLAS KC-10 EXTENDER

Wingspan:	165 ft. 4½ in.
Length:	181 ft. 7 in.
Height:	58 ft. 1 in.
Engines:	three General Electric CF6-50C2 turbofans
Engine thrust (lbs.):	52,500
Maximum T-O weight (lbs.):	590,000
Operating altitude (ft.):	33,400
Cruising speed (mph):	564
Top speed (mph):	610
Maximum range (miles):	11,500

Right: Jet-jockey's view of the KC-10 Extender and the boom that brings much-needed fuel.

An Army UH-60 Blackhawk and infantrymen.

UTILITY AND TRANSPORT HELICOPTERS

It was not until the late 1930s that practical helicopters first appeared, and they essentially remained a novelty until the 1950s. The U.S. Army had helicopters during World War II, but they were not widely used overseas because they were considered too slow for most observation missions, too delicate for combat, and too small to have the load-carrying ability to be useful as transports.

As it had been with airplanes earlier, the development of helicopters was simply a matter of figuring out what they could do before deciding what to use them for. By the Korean War, it had been determined that the limited capacity of "whirlybirds" could be helpful for such missions as search and rescue or medical evacuation.

By the 1950s, three major manufacturers had come to the forefront of American helicopter technology. Bell was building small helicopters, Sikorsky was building middle-size machines, and Piasecki (later to become Boeing Vertol) was building large transport helicopters with twin main rotors that could carry big loads. In the 1960s, the Vietnam War saw the helicopter emerge as a major weapons system in the same way that the airplane had in World War II. The Boeing Vertol CH-47 Chinook proved itself an important cargo hauler; the Sikorsky H-3 Jolly Green Giant saved many lives deep in enemy territory; and the Bell UH-1 Huey became the single most important motorized vehicle of the entire war.

The American experience in the Vietnam War was, in fact, the major factor affecting development of military helicopters in the last two decades. At the present time, medical evacuation and search and rescue are still important functions, but payload capacities of today's helicopters far exceed those of Korean War transport aircraft. Speed and agility make today's helicopters the modern equivalent of a swift cavalry horse.

The largest user of military helicopters in the world today, as always, is the U.S. Army, with nearly 9,000, or roughly double the inventory possessed by the Soviet Army. About two-thirds of these are observation and utility helicopters, about one-fifth are attack helicopters, and the balance are transports. The U.S. Navy and Marine Corps have about 400 helicopters altogether, with roughly one-half being assigned to reconnaissance or antisubmarine work, and the others about equally divided between transport and attack functions. The U.S. Air Force operates fewer than 200 helicopters, and those are mostly assigned to utility and rescue work. The U.S. Coast Guard has just over 100 helicopters, with all of them assigned to search and rescue.

The helicopter is an integral part of the *airmobile* concept that is the U.S. Army's specialty. The Soviet Army has two and a half times the personnel and four times the tanks of the U.S. Army. Thus, the U.S. Army uses the flexibility offered by a heliborne force to attempt redress of this imbalance. That the U.S. Army has chosen to put so much emphasis on the airmobile concept demonstrates how their faith in the helicopter has evolved.

Marine Reservists operate a CH-53A Sea Stallion out of NAS Dallas.

UH-1 HUEY (IROQUOIS)

More Hueys—nearly 10,000—were built than any other helicopter in history. They were to the Vietnam War what the Jeep was to World War II: the single most important piece of American hardware in the war.

The Iroquois was born in the mid-1950s when the U.S. Army began naming its helicopters for Indian tribes, but soon after it received its numeric designation, the name Iroquois was quickly forgotten. The Iroquois made its first flight in 1956 as the XH-10, but by the time production models were delivered two years later, the designation had been changed to HU-1 (Helicopter, Utility, first). Seeing the new designation stenciled on the sides, people soon began reading "HU-1" phonetically and the Iroquois has been known as "Huey" ever since.

Slated for the mundane role of routine utility helicopter, the Huey arrived in the Army's Aviation Section at a rather auspicious time, when war clouds were beginning to gather over Southeast Asia. With its eight-to-ten person capacity and its ability to carry nearly a ton of freight, the UH-1B and UH-1C were ideally suited to the requirements of the U.S. Army in Vietnam. The Army's commitment to the war increased from 14,700 troops at the end of 1964, to 116,800 a year later. Along with them came the first UH-1Ds, a Huey that was 15 feet longer, could transport 15 soldiers, and carry a half again bigger payload than the Huey it replaced.

The Huey did everything in Vietnam. For the First Air Cavalry, they were fast horses, and for most of the men wounded in action, they served as ambulances. Early in the war, Hueys were equipped with machine guns mounted on the side to be used against ground fire during rescue missions, a step that advanced the attack helicopter concept. Of the nearly 3,000 Hueys lost in this war, half were downed by ground fire.

The Huey was one vehicle about which all services could agree. With the exception of the Coast Guard, all services have been more than just casual users of the Huey, although the Army has bought far more than any-

one else. The Air Force has purchased over 200, originally for flying people from place to place on the sprawling ICBM sites of the northern plains and for utility and rescue purposes. The Navy and Marine Corps use them principally for utility and rescue purposes. The Marines have traditionally used the larger CH-46 Sea Knight in the light transport role, for which the Army has used the Huey.

Ultimately, it is planned that the Sikorsky UH-60s will replace the current Hueys, but it is also likely that the UH-1 will still be around until the next century. They certainly will be remembered as having demonstrated, more than any other helicopter, the overall practicality and versatility of using helicopters in the modern army.

BELL UH-1H HUEY (IROQUOIS)

Main rotor diameter:	48 ft.
Length of fuselage:	41 ft. 10¾ in.
Height overall:	14 ft. 5½ in.
Engine:	one Avco Lycoming T53-L-13 turboshaft
Engine (hp):	1,400
Maximum T-O weight (lbs.):	9,500
Operating altitude (ft.):	12,600
Cruising speed (mph):	127
Top speed (mph):	127
Maximum range (miles):	318

Right: In this practice manuever, a reconnaissance team rappels from a Marine UH-1N.

HH-3
JOLLY GREEN
GIANT
CH-53
SEA STALLION

If one could say that the C-130 could be a one-air-plane air force, then we could easily describe the Sikorsky H-3/H-53 series as the helicopter of choice if a whole force were to be built around a single basic type. It has had a multitude of jobs and more names than can be found in a small-town phone book.

Development of the series started in the late 1950s when the Navy required an antisubmarine helicopter. The huge SH-3 Sea King, with its 62 foot, five-blade main rotor came into being. The SH-3, and the mine-laying/minesweeping RH-3, joined the Navy in the early 1960s. It then caught the eye of the Air Force, which ordered an armed transport version under the CH-3 designation, but without the Sea King name. Deployed to Vietnam, many of the CH-3s were used for long-range, armed rescue missions deep in enemy territory, and were subsequently redesignated HH-3. Air Force pilots facing capture after being shot down over Laos or North Vietnam were relieved to see the big, olive-colored choppers coming in to rescue them, and came to call the HH-3s "Jolly Green Giants." This unofficial name became legendary.

At home, the Coast Guard also bought HH-3s for rescue work. These, being painted white rather than green, couldn't be called Jolly Green Giants, so the Coast Guard adopted the official name Pelican. The HH-3 still remains this service's standard rescue helicopter.

The relationship between the Sikorsky H-3 and H-53 series was much the same as the relationship between Boeing Vertol's CH-46 and CH-47. In each case, the second type represented an advancement over the basic type pioneered by the former. Ordered by the Marine Corps, the CH-53 first flew in 1964 and entered service two years later under the name Sea Stallion. Similar in profile to the H-3, the Sea Stallion also had two engines but its big six-blade main rotor had a diameter of over 72 feet. As it had with the earlier type, the Air Force also bought a large number for use as rescue helicopters. The Air Force HH-53 entered service in Vietnam in the summer of 1967 with the predictably obvious name "Super Jolly." The

(continued on p. 290)

Right: **America's biggest, strongest, and most sophisticated helicopter is the H-53, which is operated by the Air Force, Navy, and Marines.**

(continued from p. 288)

Navy, meanwhile, acquired some for mine-laying/mine-sweeping purposes under the RH-53 designation.

One important difference between the Air Force HH-53 and the Navy RH-53 is that the latter was designed so that its rotors could fold easily to fit into the elevator of an aircraft carrier. It was this characteristic that led to its selection as the helicopter to be used in the ill-fated attempt in April, 1980, to rescue 52 American hostages held by the Iranian government in Teheran. The mission was aborted when three of the eight RH-53s malfunctioned en route to Desert One, the initial staging area. Six helicopters had been determined to be the minimum requirement for a successful mission, so there was little that could be done to extract success from the jaws of defeat.

In 1981, the Marine Corps took delivery of the CH-53E Super Stallion, the largest type of the series and one capable of carrying 55 fully outfitted Marines. It can lift heavier loads than any other helicopter in the Western World. Two variations of the CH-53E are the Navy's mine warfare MH-53E and the Air Force MH-53H Pave Low III, which is designed for special commando operations at night and/or in adverse weather conditions. With forward-looking infrared terrain-following radar, titanium armor, and 7.62-millimeter miniguns, Pave Low IIIs are the type of equipment that would have worked at Desert One.

SIKORSKY HH-3 JOLLY GREEN GIANT

Main rotor diameter:	62 ft.
Length of fuselage:	73 ft.
Height overall:	18 ft. 1 in.
Engines:	two General Electric T-58-GE-5 turboshafts
Engine (hp):	1,500
Maximum T-O weight (lbs.):	22,050
Operating altitude (ft.):	11,100
Top speed (mph):	162
Maximum range (miles):	465

SIKORSKY CH-53 SEA STALLION

Main rotor diameter:	79 ft.
Length of fuselage:	73 ft. 4 in.
Height overall:	17 ft. 5½ in.
Engines:	two General Electric T-64-GE-416 turboshafts
Engine (hp):	4,380 (peak)
Maximum T-O weight (lbs.):	73,500
Operating altitude (ft.):	18,500
Top speed (mph):	196
Maximum range (miles):	1,290

It was a gaggle of RH-53 Sea Stallions that came to grief during the Iran hostage rescue mission.

CH-47 CHINOOK

The last of the great twin-rotor helicopters that began in the late 1940s at Piasecki, the Chinook is not particularly dashing but it is nothing short of a star workhorse for the U.S. Army.

Having first flown in 1961, the CH-47 is a sister ship to the twin-rotored CH-46 Sea Knight, which first flew in 1958. In fact, the two helicopters were originally designated HC-1A and HC-1B. The CH-47 is nearly 20 percent longer than the CH-46 and is capable of lifting two tons internally or eight tons below on an external sling. The Chinook can carry more than 40 fully equipped troops and, like the CH-46, has a large set of "barn doors" in its aft fuselage for straight-in loading.

The Chinook is a thundering, vibrating elephant, but can it lift! The CH-47 routinely hauls jeeps and small trucks as well as the new M198 155-millimeter howitzer, and it even has been known to carry a 24,750 pound Caterpillar D-5 bulldozer.

Though they were built in far fewer numbers than the ubiquitous Huey, the Chinooks were a good complement to the smaller UH-1 in Southeast Asia. They didn't have speed or maneuverability and they made a wonderful ground fire target, but they could haul large numbers of troops, lift heavy equipment, and recover downed aircraft—including bringing home entire Hueys!

In 1980, Boeing Vertol began a modernization program that will result in over 400 existing U.S. Army Chinooks being completely rebuilt and refurbished to extend their service life into the next century.

BOEING VERTOL CH-47D CHINOOK

Rotor diameter (two):	60 ft. (each)
Length of fuselage:	51 ft.
Height overall:	18 ft. 7¾ in.
Engines:	two Avco Lycoming T55-L-712 turboshafts
Engine (hp):	3,750
Maximum T-O weight (lbs.):	33,000
Operating altitude (ft.):	15,000
Cruising speed (mph):	150
Top speed (mph):	173
Maximum range (miles):	1,279

Right: **The CH-47 Chinook is the Army's biggest rotary-wing heavy lifter.**

H-60
BLACK HAWK/
NIGHT HAWK/
SEAHAWK

The UH-60 Black Hawk—the Army version of the basic H-60 helicopter—was created to fill some incredibly important shoes—those of the Huey! In the early 1970s, the U.S. Army realized that one day the Huey would be too old to fly and that it was time to start planning for a successor. What evolved has been a helicopter that is everything Huey was and more. In fact, there eventually will be a "Hawk" for every purpose to which the Huey was applied, and then some. In this sense, the Hawk family will be like miniature H-53s.

The first prototype YUH-60 flew in 1974 and was evaluated against the Boeing Vertol YUH-61 for two years. Sikorsky won the contract and delivered the first 650 UH-60 Black Hawks between 1978 and 1985.

The U.S. Air Force has *also* ordered a limited block of UH-60s, modified with booms to make them aerial refuelable, and has expressed an interest in a combat rescue variant that could operate in adverse weather, day or night. If produced, this helicopter would be designated HH-60 and would be called Night Hawk.

(continued on p. 298)

Right: **Light infantrymen rappel 100 feet to the ground from a UH-60 Blackhawk.**

(continued from p. 296)

At the same time that the Army was looking for a successor to the Huey, the Navy was looking for something called a Light Airborne Multipurpose System (LAMPS), which was a roundabout way of saying "utility helicopter with antisubmarine capability." In any case, the choice for LAMPS was a Hawk, and this being the Navy, it would, of course, be called Seahawk.

The first SH-60 Seahawks became operational with the U.S. Navy in 1984. The LAMPS SH-60s will have the primary assignment of detecting and interdicting both submarines and surface ships, although search and rescue and medical evacuation will be important secondary functions. The Seahawk is identical to the Black Hawk in overall structure, but differs significantly in its specialized electronics and avionics that are tailored to the specific needs of the mission.

The Black Hawk, meanwhile, has a repertoire of weaponry that would make a Huey pilot jealous and delight anyone who has to take one into combat. There is provision to side-mount one or two machine guns, and stubby winglets above the main cabin doors have pylons that can carry unguided rockets or up to 16 Hellfire anti-armor missiles.

The Black Hawk's baptism of fire occurred when it participated in the American invasion of Grenada in October, 1983. Black Hawks were used to land troops of the 82nd and 101st Airborne Divisions under enemy fire, and to evacuate casualties to Navy assault ships offshore. This campaign proved to be a successful initiation ritual for the U.S. Army's first utility helicopter, now bound for service well into the 21st century.

SIKORSKY H-60 BLACK HAWK/NIGHT HAWK

Main rotor diameter:	53 ft. 8 in.
Length of fuselage:	50 ft. ¾ in.
Height overall:	16 ft. 10 in.
Engines:	two General Electric T700-GE-700 turboshafts
Engine (hp):	1,560
Maximum T-O weight (lbs.):	20,250
Operating altitude (ft.):	19,000
Top speed (mph):	184
Maximum range (miles):	1,012

SIKORSKY H-60 SEAHAWK

Main rotor diameter:	53 ft. 8 in.
Length of fuselage:	50 ft. ¾ in.
Height overall:	17 ft. 1 in.
Engines:	two General Electric T700-GE-401 turboshafts
Engine (hp):	1,690
Maximum T-O weight (lbs.):	21,884
Operating altitude (ft.):	19,000
Top speed (mph):	145
Maximum range (miles):	1,012

The Army's UH-60 Blackhawk—faster and stronger than the Huey—is the successor to that chopper for troop-carrying missions.

ATTACK *HELICOPTERS*

A sunset takeoff of an
AH-1 Cobra.

The difference between *attack* helicopters and other helicopters or warplanes is that they must be seen as being *combat* aircraft with *rotary* rather than *fixed* wings. Attack helicopters are the fighters and bombers of the vertical dimension.

Before World War I, nobody had any idea of the offensive potential of airplanes. Before Vietnam, who could have visualized the helicopter as a serious *offensive* weapon? It began in 1964 with UH-1 Hueys being armed with machine guns, then progressed to the idea of creating the HueyCobra gunship, which was to become the model for all current attack helicopters.

Today, most military helicopters are capable of carrying guns. Some, such as the UH-60 Black Hawk, can even carry Hellfire missiles. The distinguishing feature of attack helicopters is that *combat* is their primary, and in most cases *only*, purpose.

As with most advanced weapons systems, the United States and the Soviet Union are the principal users of attack helicopters. The Soviets' first major type, the Mil-24 Hind, has been exported to all Warsaw Pact nations as well as such Soviet client states as Vietnam and Nicaragua. It is a heavy machine in the same size and weight class as the Sikorsky H-3. Heavily armed and armored, it is equipped with rotary cannon turrets under its nose and can carry a wide assortment of bombs and rockets. It was one of the USSR's most potent and widely used air-to-ground weapons during the war in Afghanistan. It was particularly well-suited to the mountainous terrain where land vehicles couldn't go and in steep canyons unsuited for faster, fixed-wing attack planes. However, the Hind's decade of involvement in Afghanistan highlighted some of its shortcomings, which now have been addressed by a new generation of faster and less vulnerable Soviet attack helicopters, such as the Mil-28 Havoc and Kamov Hokum, which will become operational with Soviet forces within the next decade.

In any major conflict in Europe, attack helicopters will play an important air-to-ground role, but there is also the likelihood of air-to-air combat *between* attack helicopters, a phenomena that was reported during the Iran–Iraq war but not yet documented in detail (at least publicly). While much of attack helicopter development time has been devoted to making them a potent air-to-ground weapon, the notion of defending against other gunships must now also be addressed. It was something the United States didn't have to think about in Vietnam nor the Russians in Afghanistan, but it is a consideration that should be met in the evolution of the newest genre of combat aircraft on the modern battlefield.

The AH-64 Apache is a heavy attack helicopter. It is the Army's most up-to-date and capable tank buster.

AH-1 HUEYCOBRA/ SUPERCOBRA

Like so many weapons systems, the HueyCobra was an invention born of necessity. Hueys on routine troop transport or medevac missions in Vietnam were coming under intense ground fire. They did have machine guns in the cabins, but completion of the mission came first. Eventually, somebody got the idea of sending several extra Hueys along for the sole purpose of riding shotgun on the transport Hueys. They were armed with air-to-ground rockets, as well as machine guns, and were used to counterattack sources of enemy ground fire.

Bell Helicopter, the builder of the Huey, found out what the Army aircrews were doing, and went one step further. Bell stripped the large, dozen-occupant cabin off a Huey, leaving only the tail boom, engine, rotors, and landing gear. The old cabin was then replaced with a very narrow (barely 38 inches), but armored, cabin with room for only two crew members—the pilot and a gunner. A turret with two 7.62-millimeter miniguns or one 20-millimeter rotary cannon was installed under its chin, and short, stubby winglets were placed on the side of the fuselage to carry rocket-launchers, grenade-launchers, or more guns. Thus the HueyCobra was born!

The U.S. Army bought the idea immediately, ordered 1,119 of them into production as AH-1G, and deployed

them to Vietnam by the summer of 1967. The Marine Corps, in turn, ordered 49 of a twin-engined AH-1J variant for delivery in 1969 under the name SeaCobra. After the war, the Marines ordered another 35 AH-1Js, while Iran's Shah Mohammed Reza Pahlavi ordered 202 AG-1Js for his burgeoning Imperial Army. The Marines also ordered an additional 57 updated AH-1T SeaCobras for delivery in 1977 and 44 AH-1T-Plus "SuperCobras" for delivery in 1986. These helicopters had a heavier payload, more armor, and were configured to be armed with TOW anti-armor missiles.

In 1975, the Army began buying over one thousand additional AH-1S HueyCobras, a mixed fleet of new helicopters, and about 400 modernized AH-1Gs. These, like the Marine Corps AH-1Ts, have the capability of toting

(continued on p. 306)

Right: **The Army and Marines both operate versions of the AH-1 Cobra gunship.**

(continued from p. 304)

eight TOW antitank missiles or 19 tube rocket-launchers. The gun turrets are also new and can accommodate either a 20-millimeter or 30-millimeter cannon, directed by a helmet-mounted sight. Small wonder that this helicopter appeared just after the movie *Star Wars*!

The helicopter gunship concept turned out to be one of the major successes of the Vietnam War, a war plagued by failed weapons systems. It was, in fact, probably one of the half dozen most important of such systems to have been invented *because* of the war. The concept, and the HueyCobra itself, went on to become a lasting part of the U.S. Army's arsenal and of their battlefield doctrine.

BELL AH-1G HUEYCOBRA

Main rotor diameter:	44 ft.
Length of fuselage:	53 ft. 1 in.
Height overall:	13 ft. 5 in.
Engine:	one Avco Lycoming T-53-L-703 turboshaft
Engine (hp):	1,800
Maximum T-O weight (lbs.):	10,000
Operating altitude (ft.):	12,200
Cruising speed (mph):	141
Top speed (mph):	195
Maximum range (miles):	315

BELL AH-1S SUPERCOBRA

Main rotor diameter:	48 ft.
Length of fuselage:	48 ft. 2 in.
Height overall:	14 ft. 2 in.
Engines:	two General Electric T700-GE-700 turboshafts
Engine (hp):	1,600
Maximum T-O weight (lbs.):	14,000
Operating altitude (ft.):	7,400
Cruising speed (mph):	172
Top speed (mph):	219
Maximum range (miles):	261

The AH-1 Cobra is an earlier, lighter, and less sophisticated version of the AH-64 Apache.

Left, top and bottom: The Cobra carries a three-barrel 20-millimeter cannon that is aimed with a helmet-mounted gunsight. *Right:* In addition to a cannon, the Cobra can sling a variety of bombs, rockets, and antitank missiles.

OH-6 CAYUSE/ DEFENDER

The old Hughes Helicopter Company facility at Mesa, Arizona, which McDonnell Douglas bought in 1984, is the world center of combat helicopter technology. Here, the Apache is king, but in darkened corners there lurks a little sprite whose exploits have been performed far and wide.

The Hughes Model 500 (now McDonnell Douglas Model 500) was born in the 1960s as a small commercial helicopter, and it did reasonably well. The U.S. Army took an interest in it because it was light (less than one-third the weight of an unloaded Huey), and its quickness and agility were impressive. The Army bought over 1,400 as observation helicopters under the designation OH-6 and named them Cayuse after the Indian tribe. Because they were quiet little things, the Cayuses came to be favored for counterinsurgency—and other secret operations—over the larger, noisier Huey. The OH-6 can carry only four people, but special missions rarely require more.

After the Vietnam War, it was interesting to watch the Model 500 evolve along two tracks. On one hand, it was developed into a commercially marketed product, and on the other, it became a hush-hush, secret weapon. Not surprisingly, many of its buyers were foreign military, paramilitary, and police organizations.

Marketed today under the name Defender, the Model 500 is so small that it appears to be overwhelmed by the weapons and electronic gear with which it can be configured. These include a 7.62-millimeter machine gun, four-teen 2.75-inch rockets, or a 40-millimeter grenade launcher. An antiship version, used by Taiwan, can carry two torpedoes and all the sensors necessary to locate submarines or enemy surface ships up to 170 miles from the mother ship. Four TOW missile tubes turn the little Defender into a potent antitank weapon, which is now in use in both South Korea and Israel. Such anti-aircraft missiles as the Stinger, combined with the "Black Hole" infrared suppression system, help keep the Defender safe.

U.S. Army Model 500MD Defenders were the first aircraft to enter Grenada during the October 1983 invasion. They went in with the special operations commandos and, as such, their exploits have never been officially acknowledged or publicly discussed. In fact, they flew only during the first night and are remembered from just a tiny handful of fuzzy photos. When Operation Urgent Fury became an overt, rather than a covert, operation, the Defenders withdrew quietly.

(continued on p. 313)

Right: **The OH-6 Cayuse is a light-duty battlefield observation helicopter that was widely used in Vietnam.**

(continued from p. 310)

In 1987 and 1988 United States forces were sent to the Persian Gulf to escort oil tankers that were being harassed by Iranian air and sea forces. Though they are an Army (rather than Navy or Marine Corps) weapon, the Defenders were sent out aboard U.S. Navy ships to apply their special talents to the situation.

Because they can operate at night as easily as most helicopters can operate in daylight, and because they are able to fly just a few feet above water or land, Defenders are ideal for patrol missions. Their quiet operation and impressive defensive electronics also make them very stealthy, and their torpedoes and TOW missiles make them the literal nightmare of every prowling Iranian gunboat.

The OH-6 Cayuse is still in service, but it is a bird of a different era. Its younger sibling, however, has only just begun an intriguing life on the front lines of counterterrorism. Yet, the remarkable Defender would not have been possible without the Cayuse.

Someday, when the tight-lipped security surrounding the deployment of the Defender to Grenada and the Persian Gulf is lifted, there'll be a tale to be told. Until then—which may well be the end of the century—there will be whispered stories of the daring exploits of a little gnat of a helicopter that can sting like a scorpion and disappear like a puff of smoke.

McDONNELL DOUGLAS OH-6 DEFENDER

Main rotor diameter:	27 ft. 4 in.
Length of fuselage:	23 ft. 11 in.
Height overall:	8 ft. 10¾ in.
Engine:	one Allison 250-C3 turboshaft
Engine (hp):	425
Maximum T-O weight (lbs.):	3,100
Operating altitude (ft.):	16,600
Cruising speed (mph):	132
Top speed (mph):	140
Maximum range (miles):	233

Right: **The OH-6 Cayuse is a light-duty battlefield observation helicopter that was widely used in Vietnam.**

AH-64
APACHE

They sneak in low over the salmon-colored mesas that ripple in the hot Arizona sun. They come silently, treacherously, and armed to the teeth. It's the Apaches!

But today, "Geronimo" is a call sign, not an enemy combat commander. We're not living in the 1880s, and the Apaches in question are the first helicopters in the world to have been developed *strictly* for the purpose of combat.

The first of over 600 operational Apaches joined the Army in 1984, and a year later made a deployment flight of over 1,100 miles. This demonstrated that it is possible for Apaches to make the flight to Europe from the United States under their own power, if other transport were not available. When other air transport *is* available, a pair of AH-64s could fit neatly into a C-141 and *six* could be carried by a C-5.

Once the enemy is in sight, the Apache has a remarkable array of weapons available. Start with a 30-millimeter Gatling gun firing ten rounds of high explosive ammunition per second, and then add winglets with pylons for 16 Hellfire antitank missiles or 76 folding fin aerial rockets! There is even a capability for AIM-9 Sidewinder air-to-air missiles for fighting warplanes or other helicopter gunships.

As in the HueyCobra, the gunner sits low in an armored seat in the forward cockpit, with the pilot behind and above him. Forward-looking infrared (FLIR) is available to provide a clear view in zero visibility during low-level dashes through rugged terrain.

In the 19th century, the Apache was the last Indian tribe to hold out against the white man. Geronimo's small band lived off the land and fought on for many years after all other major tribes had capitulated. In a future conflict, their namesake may well face similar challenges. Outnumbered in a hostile environment, the AH-64 would have to survive with sparse or nonexistent support facilities, hitting and running, wearing down the enemy with various unexpected blows, then fading away into the night, to feel their way down a narrow canyon by infrared light. In the worlds of both conventional and unconventional warfare, the attack helicopter concept has earned a cherished place. The Apache has arrived to take its own position at the head of the line.

McDONNELL DOUGLAS AH-64 APACHE

Main rotor diameter:	48 ft.
Length of fuselage:	48 ft. 2 in.
Height overall:	11 ft. 6½ in.
Engines:	two General Electric T700-GE-701 turboshafts
Engine (hp):	1,696
Maximum T-O weight (lbs.):	17,333
Operating altitude (ft.):	21,000
Cruising speed (mph):	177
Top speed (mph):	184
Maximum range (miles):	1,057

Right: **The Apache is operated by a crew of two, with the pilot in the raised rear cockpit and the weapons operator up front.**

An Apache in a high-speed, low-level flight at Ft. Hood, Texas.

From top, first and second photos: Sensors and television fill the AH-64's nose; the pilot's view at night. *Third and fourth photos:* A 30-millimeter gun is linked to the gunmen's helmet-mounted sight. The weapon moves with the gunner's head. *Right:* A wide angle view of the AH-64.

The complex Apache is expensive in unit cost and maintenance hours.